Frame Publishers
Amsterdam

Birkhäuser –
Publishers for Architecture
Basel / Boston / Berlin

Introduction
Eating: A Global Experience 004

Intentionallies
Linc Styles Café 010

Giant Design
Buddha Boy 020

Mental Industrial Design
Dahlberg 030

Karim Rashid
Askew 040

Ippolito Fleitz Group
Trattoria da Lorreta 050

Jason Caroline Design
Kushiyaki 060

Maurice Mentjens
Witloof 070

Torii Design Office
Hitsuji 080

Hawkins\Brown
OQO 090

Andrea Lupacchini Architect
Glass 100

A00 Architecture
a FuturePerfect 110

Claudio Colucci Design
Delicabar 120

Estudio Minim Vilá & Blanch
El Bosque de Samsung 130

Rockwell Group
Kittichai 140

Maurice Mentjens
Thaiphoon 150

Francesc Rifé
Nuba 160

Puresang
Ciné Città 170

SHH Associates
The hub 180

Jason Jenkins & The Finevibe
Kantinery 190

George Henry Chidiac Architects
Café Blanc 200

Steve Leung Designers and
Alan Chan Design Company
MX 210

Khosla Associates and tsk Design
Khyber 220

RaiserLopesDesigners
Olio e Pane 230

Abelardo Gonzalez Arkitektbyrå
World Hockey Bar 240

Marcel Wanders Studio
Thor 250

Costa Group
Mc Donald's 260

Hashimoto Yukio Design Office
Kamonka Ueno Bamboo Garden 270

Slick Design & Manufacturing
Carnevor 280

Stefan Zwicky Architect and Müller
und Fleischli
Food Hall globus du Molard 290

Leigh & Orange
Isola Bar & Grill 300

Mueller Kneer Associates
The Cotton House 310

PrastHooft Architects
Brasserie Harkema 320

Simone Micheli
P Food & Wine 330

IDing
Odeon 340

Andrés Escobar & Associés
Duvet 350

Addresses restaurants
and project credits 361

Addresses
architects 372

Addresses
photographers 374

Colophon 376

Eating: A Global Experience

by Shonquis Moreno

The reason I never learned to cook is that I moved to New York City at the age of 17. Why dirty dishes, schlep groceries, cook for one and eat alone when you can give yourself an international culinary and cultural education and enjoy yourself at the same time? People have been eating out for millennia. Archaeological evidence tells us there were street vendors and takeaway shops from biblical Ur to ancient Athens and Pompeii. In the late 13th century, Marco Polo found Hangzhou, China, bustling with sophisticated restaurants that offered individual seating, cutlery and waiters who memorized and recited a menu and juggled dishes between kitchen and dining room. By the 15th century, Japan, too, boasted similar establishments. It was the advent of coffee and the coffee house during the 17th century that brought the notion of 'drinking out' (a prelude to 'eating out') to Europeans. It wasn't until the mid-18th century that French shops began to serve a broth called a restaurant (meaning a 'restorative'). Within the next 100 years, the word had come to refer to the establishment itself instead of to the dish it served. The first truly modern restaurant in the West, Paris's La Grande Taverne de Londres, opened in 1782 at a time when menus were growing longer and more complex and competition among chefs, who sought far and wide for inspiration, was growing fiercer. In cities around the world today, restaurants provide the first access to other cultures; going out to eat is the cheapest, safest way to travel the world. Architects currently designing restaurants must not only address fundamental functions (highly trafficked interiors that include, at the least, a dining room, kitchen, lavatories, service areas and circulation for waitstaff); they must also cater to our search for something out of the ordinary. There's no doubt that restaurants must offer good food, but good food is no longer the be-all and end-all in competitive economies where diners are glutted with choice. Architects must provide an experience.

ARCHAEOLOGICAL EVIDENCE TELLS US THERE WERE STREET VENDORS AND TAKEAWAY SHOPS FROM BIBLICAL UR TO ANCIENT ATHENS AND POMPEII.

Sometimes the experience is a rudimentary social one: in 2001, Diller + Scofidio's design of Brasserie in the windowless cellar of Mies van der Rohe's glassy Seagram Tower made explicit the fact that restaurants and bars give city people the opportunity to both see and be seen. Cameras strung above Brasserie's bar capture images of entering clientele on a necklace of monitors. 'Spaces are always performative whether they have moving parts or not, so architecture is about events,' Diller said at the time.

It's the intersection of inert material form with bodies in a context where people perform activities that makes architecture into an event.' In 2005, architect Yukio Hashimoto played up architecture as an event in his design of Tokyo's Kamonka Ueno Bamboo Garden, which surrounds visitors with layers of latticework that suggest a grove of bamboo. By dividing an open-plan interior into porous zones, Hashimoto gives diners a glimpse of the scene around them and a sense of privacy. He also provides a dramatic path into the restaurant through a series of illuminated keyhole-shaped portals and compares this built structure to the story line of a novel or film. 'The passage holds many subplots,' Hashimoto says, 'and sometimes paints a picture of how the story of the visit will end.'

GOING OUT TO EAT IS THE CHEAPEST, SAFEST WAY TO TRAVEL THE WORLD.

At other times the experience that restaurant architects provide is simply about relaxation and wellbeing – and the materials used to narrate their stories can vary from warm woods to high-tech plastics. A series of prototype interiors designed by Costa Group for fast-food behemoth McDonald's in Italy last year pointedly departs from the usual frenetic, un-upholstered, vinyl-and-laminate-clad McDonald's interior. The McCafé, where one wall is stacked with cracked wooden beams and a whorled wood sculpture, has the warmth of a local coffee house and evokes the comfort of a living room. The emphasis on relaxation was an effort 'to counteract the outside frenzy', says Costa architect Luigi Benvenuti. Likewise, in Hong Kong, Steve Leung Designers and Alan Chan Design Company embedded TV screens into the tabletops of an eatery called MX, responding to the local habit of dining telly-side in an effort to make patrons feel, almost literally, at home.

At the opposite end of the spectrum, many people like to leave home in a dramatic way when they dine out. The best restaurant design today allows diners to take a journey, without travelling, to a place they don't know or to escape from a place they know all too well. The Rockwell Group's 2004 New York design for Kittichai announces a change of geography at the entrance to the bar, where a column rising from the stained-wood floor wears the coarse armature of a coconut tree. Between each ring of 'bark', a strip of light shines upward. Flowers held captive in jar-lined shelves are the plum orchids so ubiquitous in Thailand that their colours adorn the Thai flag.

Transporting the diner to places unknown is only one strategy used to entertain. While design must express the personality of the brand, food, culture or chef, it must also surprise, provoke or captivate us without becoming overwhelming. Sometimes, oddly enough, this is achieved most conspicuously in the toilets. In 2001, the most salient feature of Thomas Leeser's Glass lounge was a voyeuristic façade that exposed the restaurant's unisex rest room as people soaped up and reapplied lipstick in mirrors above the sinks; another of his Manhattan designs placed a sheer-walled lavatory at the centre of the restaurant. Leigh & Orange's 2004 Isola Bar & Grill is Hong Kong's largest Western restaurant. Visitors to the toilet will find either blood-red walls embossed with a crocodile-skin pattern or glazed, water-filled ceilings. In New York's freshly minted mega-restaurant Morimoto (Frame 49), Tadao Ando recently designed white lavatory stalls backed with infinity mirrors filled with wisteria, maple leaves, and plum and cherry blossoms. The stall doors, washed with a milky urethane, appear to glow slightly, while guests inside are transported into a dimly lit dreamscape. One of the strengths of Ando's design is that every spot in this Japanese restaurant holds a small moment of placelessness and surprise.

Providing a luxurious environment is one of the easiest (and most costly) ways to entertain guests. Near Morimoto in Manhattan's Meatpacking District is Buddakan by Christian Liaigre, another mega-restaurant that opened in the spring of 2006. In a bid to conjure opulence, Liaigre made stunning use of lofty spaces while playing with a variety of scales (from Versailles-esque halls to the intimacy of a bar mimicking a small library). This approach emphasizes one of the fundamental functions of the restaurant: to provide a seamless experience that exists in the service of all our senses, and it's this essential 'ingredient' that calls on the architect to be a good cook.

'In the Morimoto and Buddakan restaurants,' says New York-based Stephanie Goto of Goto Designs, who served as the creative director on both projects, 'there was a conscious attention to the overall experience. It is not just about the food or design elements of the space, but about how the food smells, tastes, looks – while you see, touch, and feel the space. The creation of the space is like a chef combining the perfect ingredients.' Goto stresses the need for an broad design vision in which each element is carefully considered and the stage is set for a performance that relies on a narrative that ties it all together.

Storytelling. Most architects don't have such copious amounts of space or money as Liaigre with which to concoct the fantasy. But, as the architects at Lewis.Tsuramaki.Lewis (LTL) have made clear in several recent restaurant designs, limitations often inspire innovation. At the tiny seafood boite Tides *(Frame 46)*, the clever use of a humble instrument for eating – the bamboo skewer, or rather, 120,000 skewers that pierce the ceiling – creates a patterned shag that resembles a swaying bed of sea grass and allows a beautiful composition to obscure the limitations of the 39-m2 space. 'The most significant issue for architectural design,' says Paul Lewis of LTL, 'is to be simultaneously utterly pragmatic and unprecedented. This schizophrenia or oscillation between efficiency, usually located in the architectural plan, and extraordinary effects, often lodged in the thick surfaces of the walls and ceiling, is what characterizes our restaurant work. A client can know and demand the former but cannot, by definition, specify the latter. An efficient restaurant plan is a product of experience, whereas delirious plays between materials and form must be invented.'

IT IS NOT JUST ABOUT THE FOOD OR DESIGN ELEMENTS OF THE SPACE, BUT ABOUT HOW THE FOOD SMELLS, TASTES, LOOKS – WHILE YOU SEE, TOUCH, AND FEEL THE SPACE.

Material, form, texture, light and colour are crucial tools in the dream-making of restaurant design. Even if the story being told in a space is more abstract than straightforward, the evocation of place or mood plays as significant a role today as that of cutlery and china. Colour sets the scene in the 2005 design of El Bosque de Samsung in Barcelona, where Elina Vilá and Agnès Blanch of Estudio Minim Vilá & Blanch have created an industrial-era forest. After bathing the entire space in vivid green paint, they lit the dining room with a branching canopy of fluorescent tubes. Although it was not the designers' explicit intention, the colour scheme of Manhattan's Askew restaurant seems to complement the palette of the playful international tapas on offer, an appetizing array of oranges, pinks and tart greens. Askew's design also experiments with a composition gone askew, making the space both exuberant and intimate. Planes that are not quite horizontal or vertical give diners a feeling of imbalance by scattering angled surfaces throughout the interior. Both colour and this unusual orientation whisk visitors out of the ordinary world and dislocate them for a while. On the other hand, texture is what architect George Chidiac used to anchor diners in Beirut's Café Blanc.

By creating a series of panels, he balanced the contradictions that characterize the restaurant: he located the space in the traditional Lebanese context of its food while establishing it as being wholly modern. He partitioned the interior, without eliminating its depth and porosity, by creating 1-x-1-m modules in four patterns – made from computer-cut, plaster-coated MDF– which, when rotated, can be positioned to form 16 patterns across walls and ceilings. Chidiac's panels, manufactured by the most modern of methods, nonetheless recall traditional local dwellings in which entire families lived in a single room, carving openings into thick walls made of mud and rubble in a way that embroidered them with niches suitable for storage. By combining longstanding native materials and effects with modern techniques, Chidiac, like many of the architects in this book, took the best of the old and made it new. Designers of the following projects deftly avoided the tropes of the conventional restaurant. They honoured the traditions and places from which these businesses and their menus grew, but updated them to allow the culture in question to take its place in the modern world and, not least, to give restaurant-goers a better life in the 21st century.

Intentionallies:
Linc Styles Café

40m²

LINC STYLES

13

14

Architect:
Intentionallies

Project:
Linc Styles Café

Location:
Hiroshima, Japan

Year of completion:
2004

Architect: Intentionallies
Project: Linc Styles Café
Location: Hiroshima, Japan

Text by Masaaki Takahashi
Photography by Nacása & Partners

Linc Styles Café, with its muted natural tones and soft lighting, can be found hidden away in the head office of a Hiroshima company specializing in audiovisual goods, theatre equipment and security systems for domestic use. The firm handles each project from start to finish, offering a range of services from consulting and design to the marketing and installation of its high-end products.

A spiral staircase at ground level takes visitors down to a shop selling an eclectic range of funky Japanese merchandise: electronic items, innovative consumer goods and lifestyle accessories. The café is on the second floor, and the third floor houses a home-theatre showroom, where prospective customers can browse before getting a taste of the real thing in another, purpose-designed room. Wanting to transform these three floors into a launch pad for innovative design – a place where visitors could find inspiring concepts for any number of lifestyles – the firm asked the designers at Tokyo-based Intentionallies to come up with an appropriate look. Headed by Shuwa Tei, Intentionallies is active in the fields of architecture, interior design and the design of products, from household appliances to stationery.

Preceding spread: A door handle of rough-hewn wood contrasts with the glazed entrance doors.
Opposite: A Linc Styles shop is on the first floor, the café is on the second, and a home-theatre showroom occupies the fourth floor.

Left: A square recess in the façade features a cut-out of the logo, which stands out at night.
Right: Visitors feel at home in a rustic atmosphere generated by teak flooring and wood furniture.

16

Architect:
Intentionallies

Project:
Linc Styles Café

Location:
Hiroshima, Japan

Year of completion:
2004

Given the fact that Shuwa's older brother is chart-topping DJ and musician Towa Tei (formerly a member of Deee-Lite), it's not surprising that the designer has more than a smattering of knowledge about music and digital imaging. What's more, as manager of Hanamiduki, a Harajuku restaurant that he both planned and designed, this multitalented guy was certainly capable of coming up with the goods for Linc Styles.

The designers envisioned a café that would be used not only by the shop and showroom customers, but also by the general public. Their target market was identified as thirty-somethings with a sense of style and a strong awareness of their own tastes. Intentionallies modelled the space along the lines of a tree-shaded lounge, a concept that would express the identity not only of the building but also of the company as a whole.

Aiming for a comfortably relaxing space, the designers kept the interior deliberately low-tech in order to create a contrast between the café and the firm's technologically sophisticated home-theatre products. The desired 'primitive feel' was achieved with teak flooring, as well as with a wall carved by Javanese craftsmen and clad in stone inlays whose pictographic reliefs refer to ancient Japanese family crests. Intentionallies had first experimented with this approach in a lounge at Tokyo's Hotel Claska, a boutique hotel that has made waves for its emphasis on high-quality design. Like Linc Styles Café, Claska's lounge features customized timber, as well as many pieces of furniture designed in collaboration with Southeast Asian artisans. This relaxed style, which hints at the Orient without conjuring up the atmosphere of any one country, is one that Shuwa Tei's designers have made their own.

A solid wood table at the centre of Linc Styles Café forms a massive hub which is surrounded by individually shaped stools, each carved from a single block of wood. Certain privileges make the place feel like a home away from home.

17

Above: Guests can take their drinks into the home-theatre, where modular seating can be arranged as desired.

For instance, customers may take their meals into the theatre showroom and are invited to bring in CDs and records to listen to while enjoying favourites such as the 'waffle, drink and yoghurt' combo or a dish of vanilla ice cream topped with tart strawberry sauce. The café also serves pasta and other dishes, and the drinks menu offers a good selection of Belgian beers. 'Fusion cuisine' of this sort, which is something of a rarity in Hiroshima, has helped enhance the popularity of this stylish venue.

The home-theatre showroom can be rented for a variety of functions. Seating up to 15 people, it is available for private screenings of any film the cinema buff brings along to share with friends or business associates. A seven-channel, 305-cm screen takes up an entire wall at one end of the room, producing images of incredible resolution and intensity.

Shuwa Tei's personal aspirations include gallery and hotel design, while others have suggested that he try his hand at designing holiday villas on Pacific islands such as Bali. To run a hotel, it is vital to have a thorough knowledge of the service industry, and Tei feels that his experience in café and restaurant design and management would prove to be an asset were he to follow their advice. 'A designer who's content to make a meal from fast food bought in a convenience store,' he warns, 'is not one who can make a success of a top hotel or restaurant.'

THE DESIRED 'PRIMITIVE FEEL' IS SEEN IN TEAK FLOORING AND IN A WALL CARVED BY JAVANESE CRAFTSMEN AND CLAD IN STONE INLAYS WHOSE PICTOGRAPHIC RELIEFS REFER TO JAPANESE FAMILY CRESTS.

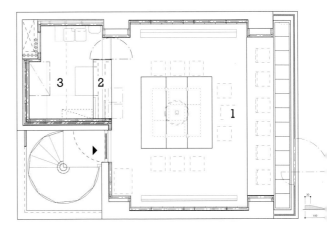

Architect:	Project:	Location:	Year of completion:
Intentionallies	Linc Styles Café	Hiroshima, Japan	2004

19

Floor plan
1 Dining area
2 Bar
3 Kitchen

The use of recycled stone and wood in the café
gives the space a warm ambience.

Giant Design and
Nerida Orsatti Design:
Buddha Boy

24

Architect:
Giant Design

Project:
Buddha Boy

Location:
Sydney, Australia

Year of completion:
2005

Architect: Giant Design
Project: Buddha Boy
Location: Sydney, Australia

Text by Shonquis Moreno
Photography by Andrew Worrsam

'Just give me noodles,' says English architect Ed Kenny of Giant Design. 'I could eat Thai noodles till they come out of my ears.' No small statement, that. And it gives even greater weight to Kenny's summary of the design of Buddha Boy, a 40-seat, 65-m2, fast-food Thai eatery that opened in December 2005 in the Parramatta shopping mall. 'Thai food,' says Kenny, 'never looked so sexy.'

Despite its small size and limited budget (€142,952), Buddha Boy brings the inner city to Sydney's expanding periphery through the use of 'one grand gesture' that maximizes the impact of the design. This gesture takes the form of walls that ribbon upwards to form a ceiling made from curved, perforated, wood panels that allow pinpoints of light to penetrate from behind. Kenny envisioned the tiny restaurant, where visitors order at a counter and sit at a communal table or in individual seats facing the wall, as 'an urban temple, a respite from the visual noise of a shopping mall'. The materials he selected work in combination with rich graphic elements from Nerida Orsatti Design, to engender a space that is thoroughly modern – in composition, palette, forms and materials, including the waitstaff uniforms – yet evocative of Thai tradition, culture and cuisine.

Preceding spread: The 40-seat, 65-m² space was envisioned as an urban temple – a respite from the hustle and bustle of the shopping mall in which it is situated.
Left: The design of fast-food Thai eatery Buddha Boy consists of a single grand gesture. At the rear of the space, a larger-than-life seated Buddha is painted in pixels of gold.

Perforated panels, which ribbon up walls and ceiling, wear a storm-cherry veneer facing.
Left: Bespoke pendants sandwich bare bulbs between yellow acrylic discs.
Right: Fully exposed to passers-by, the space looks like a brown cavern outlined by a glossy white half-arch.

'THAI FOOD NEVER LOOKED SO SEXY.'

Ed Kenny

This admixture of old and new and of urban and traditional is reflected in the name of the business which was, unusually, selected by the designers.

From the pavement, the fully exposed Buddha Boy pops onto the eyes through the broad mouth of a gleaming, bright white half-arch. 'The gloss-white façade accentuates the dark curved panels inside,' Kenny explains, 'making the contrast to surrounding shops even greater.' Breaching the arch, visitors find themselves in a cosy brown cavern accented with gold. On the right side, a menu is embedded flush in a door leading into a cupboard. Farther inside, the cash register and ordering counter front the kitchen, of which very little is visible from the dining area. Instead, drawing the gaze rapidly to the back of the space and providing an emphatic focal point, a larger-than-life seated Buddha is painted in pixels of gold. 'The Buddha is abstract,' says Kenny, calling the work 'an obscure pixelated image that reveals itself only at second glance'. And from afar. The temple theme follows through to the graphic identity of the project. Developed especially for Buddha Boy are the hand-cut letters of the logo. Derived from Thai characters, they possess the threadlike nature of traditional Thai script. Exterior signage, also reflective of the architect's big-impact tactics, is oversized to get attention fast. What makes this strategy work, however, is not just the scale – which, like neon, could become merely obnoxious and overwhelming – but also the well-considered composition of the typeface designed by Orsatti. Piled and placed throughout the restaurant, within the sight and grasp of all who enter, are menus printed with an image of the seated Buddha Boy; viewed with a little imagination, they can almost be seen as small statues of Buddha, which is what the architect intended. Whereas the menus are a tongue-in-cheek translation of something very traditional in Thai culture, however, the wholly modern waitstaff uniforms have the urban feel of the street.

Architect:	Project:	Location:	Year of completion:
Giant Design	Buddha Boy	Sydney, Australia	2005

27

Opposite: The hand-cut letters of the logo are derived from Thai characters. Menus piled on a golden plinth running the length of the common table resemble small statues of Buddha.

This page: Waitstaff uniforms have a contemporary street feel. Nerida Orsatti Design was responsible for graphic elements used throughout the space, including those featured on the uniforms.

28

Architect:
Giant Design

Project:
Buddha Boy

Location:
Sydney, Australia

Year of completion:
2005

Outfits that young people might wear the world over, they include brown T-shirts screen-printed with the pixelated Buddha Boy identity and brown-and-white trucker caps paired with trainers and jeans. All elements weave together to create a distinct identity that avoids the typical tropes of a Thai restaurant.

In the dining area, charcoal-coloured, ring-shaped Cero stools by Space Furniture echo the girth of the Buddha's belly behind them. (As rubbing the belly of a Buddha statue is supposed to bring good luck, a series of bellies seems especially auspicious.) The floor is faced in a warm brown vitrified tile, while walls and ceiling are sheathed in richly grained, perforated panels featuring storm-cherry veneer facing. Fluorescent strip lights at the base of the panels cast light subtly up the wall. Crowning the space, however, are bespoke light fixtures by Giant Design: these jubilant pendants reveal bare bulbs between yellow acrylic discs.

'The golden light from the acrylic washes the dark interior and creates strange reflections as you look through the lights,' says Kenny. 'They also reinforce the concept of the pinpoint holes in the wall panels, together with the pixels of the Buddha.' Also extending the richness of the gilt detailing is a plinth sheathed in gold leaf that runs down the centre of the wood table (custom-made by a joiner to the specifications of Giant Design), breaking its surface in a single line like the central reserve of a road – suggesting both a spiritual and a culinary path which, for some of us, are parts of the same whole – and drawing the eye, again, to the rear of the store, always back to Buddha.

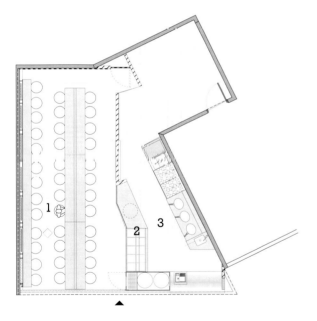

Floor plan
1 Dining area
2 Bar
3 Kitchen

Opposite: Visitors sit on charcoal-coloured, ring-shaped Cero stools by Space Furniture.

Mental Industrial Design:
Dahlberg

34

Architect:
Mental Industrial Design

Project:
Dahlberg

Location:
Helsingborg, Sweden

Year of completion:
2006

Architect: Mental Industrial Design
Project: Dahlberg
Location: Helsingborg, Sweden

Text by Chris Scott
Photography by Fredrik Segerfalk

Per Dahlberg, one of Sweden's better creators of haute cuisine, has had great success in Helsingborg with Restaurant Gastro and Café Fredriksal. His latest venture also enhances this small southern Swedish city, which is in the process of changing its image, profiling itself as an innovative urban hub and a place committed to modern design.

Dahlberg's new restaurant-café is part of Hotel Helsingborg, a monumental bank building erected in 1899 and converted into a hotel in 1930. The grand Jugendstil design of this impressive building is still intact, both inside and out. Dahlberg welcomed the challenge presented by this project. After analysing the existing situation, he opted for something totally different. To help him develop the concept, he sought out a like-minded person: designer Niklas Madsen, the founder of MIND (Mental Industrial Design), a young and dynamic company that satisfies its clients' needs with solutions beyond their expectations. The successful collaboration between Dahlberg and Madsen is, as they put it, 'all about the experience, the food and the design'. Madsen credits Dahlberg with 'designing the food that goes with my ideas'.

35

Preceding spread: Inspired by the wealth of nature, Madsen used an abundance of wood in his design.
Opposite: The door in the background leads to the hotel, where the toilets are located.

Left: The bar ends at an open kitchen that allows guests to watch as their meals are being prepared.
Right: Tables designed for Dahlberg have black Formica tabletops.

The inspiration came from London's 'gastropubs'. Dahlberg describes the phenomenon as one in which a top chef 'takes over an old pub and turns it into a gourmet restaurant with a hip interior'. The objective is to deliver quality to the customer at all levels: food, design, dining experience and sensory stimulation. Surrounded by the aroma of exquisite cuisine and a visually provocative setting, guests taste the dishes served while listening to a variety of music supplied by the designer and his DJ partner – all within a relatively small space, for the 80-m2 restaurant, with its 10-m-long bar, can serve only 30 diners at one time.

Inspired by the wealth of nature that is everywhere one looks in this part of the world, Madsen integrated lots of wood into his design, including the extensive use of teak for walls, shelves and bar; and dark-brown oiled oak from Africa for the floor. In keeping with Dahlberg's desire for

'something different', Madsen went for the unlikely colour of green, again prompted by nature but, even more so, by a reaction to 'the norm'. Extensive research had shown him that green is hardly ever found in restaurant environments. Apparently, green is a difficult colour to use, not only for interiors but also for fashion and graphic design, not to mention food. His choice has proved to be effective, however.

Other influences came from two hip hotels steeped in luxury: the Hudson in New York and the Delano in Miami Beach, both designed by Philippe Starck. Particularly struck by the dreamlike, surrealist quality of these places, Madsen endeavoured to incorporate this feeling into the Hotel Helsingborg project, along with yet another motivating force: his love of the dramatic mood expressed by the interiors of old churches.

36

Architect:
Mental Industrial Design

Project:
Dahlberg

Location:
Helsingborg, Sweden

Year of completion:
2006

Opposite left: Jenny Sjögren and Niklas Madsen designed the chandeliers, which are made from laser-cut steel sporting a coat of glossy black car paint.

Opposite right: Black Plexiglas lamps are a design by Niklas Madsen.
This page: Diners lounging on the sofa have a view of the kitchen through the green-glass part of the bar.

38

Architect:
Mental Industrial Design

Project:
Dahlberg

Location:
Helsingborg, Sweden

Year of completion:
2006

Ultimately, the new restaurant was to combine elements as diverse as nature, luxury, surrealism and religious awe.

Green glass doors and panels contrast with the palest of grey walls, a striking black ceiling and black neo-rococo chandeliers designed especially for the restaurant. Ventilation ducts, also in black, add to the dramatic effect and help to emphasize the height of the room, which is 4.5 m from floor to ceiling. Madsen was also responsible for the majority of the furniture and fittings, with the exception of the black and green chairs, Rialto 437 models from Swedish company NC Möbler; spotlights made by Modular Lighting Instruments; and, in the dishwashing room area, crystal chandeliers manufactured by Krebs of Stockholm.

Having enjoyed eating at restaurants that allow diners to watch the chef at work, Dahlberg and Madsen positioned the kitchen at the centre of the space, even opening this area to guests who want to wander in, observe the activities at close hand, and enjoy the sight and smell of their dinners being prepared. This particular feature of the interior is both a visual and olfactory stimulus.

Daring to take the 'something different' concept a step forward, Madsen came up with the idea of exposing the dishwashing room area. After much discussion, the designer persuaded Dahlberg to embrace this upfront proposal and to allow him to separate the bar from the dishwashing room by nothing more than a glass wall.

From early morning until late at night the mood changes, most notably in the evening when light radiating from black chandeliers fills the space with a glowingly celestial atmosphere. Restaurateur and designer hope that visitors to the restaurant will be touched by the drama and grandeur of the space, and that their senses will be awakened, sharpened and delighted by the Dahlberg experience.

INSPIRED BY THE WEALTH OF NATURE THAT IS EVERYWHERE ONE LOOKS IN THIS PART OF THE WORLD, NIKLAS MADSEN INTEGRATED LOTS OF WOOD INTO HIS DESIGN, INCLUDING THE EXTENSIVE USE OF TEAK FOR WALLS, SHELVES AND BAR.

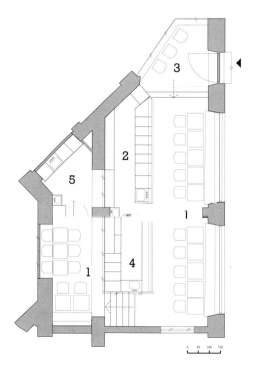

39

Floor plan
1 Dining area
2 Bar
3 Lounge
4 Kitchen
5 Dishwashing room

Opposite: Guests who climb the illuminated staircase next to the open kitchen reach a small dining area on the balcony.

HOMEMA
POPPY-S
GNOCCH
CAULIFL
PUREE S
FAVA BE
AND SPE

44

Designer: Project: Location: Year of completion
Karim Rashid   Askew   New York, USA   2005

Designer: Karim Rashid
Project: Askew
Location: New York, USA

Text by Shonquis Moreno
Photography by Tom Vack

Certain things inside Askew are, as the name suggests, slightly askew. But just slightly. You wonder – after your first martini at this diminutive bar and restaurant that opened in November 2005 in Manhattan's Noho neighbourhood – if the out-of-sync feeling might just be you. But no. Once again, it is Karim Rashid. Rashid and his cheerful minions are responsible for Askew, a project they approached in their usual manically, prolifically exuberant way. All modifiers intended.

Askew is a restaurant modelled after an izakaya, a traditional Japanese pub that invites guests to pop in for a quick bite or to linger and snack as long as they like. Although not the case at all, the colour scheme of the interior seems to deliberately match, handbag-to-shoes, the palette of executive chef Chris Lim's playful international tapas – beets and red cabbage with goat cheese, Asian pears, sour orange glazes, crabmeat cannelloni – an appetizing array of oranges and pinks and tart greens. 'We did not want to use the same palette used in so many restaurants,' insists space director Dennis Askins. 'We wanted a more contemporary and fresh feel.' Lim and Rashid are contemporary, fresh and well-matched. It's clear that their work shares the same precocious whimsy.

Preceding spread and opposite: Modelled after the Izakaya – the name given to a traditional Japanese pub – Askew is marked by crisp colours, skewed lines and the signature organic forms associated with Karim Rashid.

Left and right: On entering Askew, visitors find a long, angular, chartreuse bar lined with Arp Stools by puredesign/ OFFI, as well as a work of art, lit from behind, that resembles a band of blurred flowers.

Askew doesn't give up its secrets from the street. Upon entering, visitors are met by a long angular bar in glossy chartreuse (lined with Arp stools by puredesign/OFFI) and, in gleeful contrast, a narrow strip of artwork, lit from behind, that looks like blurred scarlet gerberas against a dark ground. Rashid stained the existing wood floors dark brown and kept the original white penny tiles. He dressed the tabletops in a bespoke, graphic, pink-and-red-flowered laminate by Folia and hemmed them with Magis's Butterfly chairs. The standout, however, is Rashid's own Digital Nature wallpaper in lime green, which he designed a few years ago for Wolf-Gordon. At Askew, the wallpaper backs the bar and most walls. Thus, using colour and form, Rashid created an exuberant interior that is simultaneously intimate by virtue of its size: only 83 m². (Those with strong views on real estate in New York City might substitute another word for 'virtue'.) Just as significant but less salient than the stature and complexion of Askew is the subtle and slightly intoxicating game – whether you know the source or not – that Rashid plays with our eyes and with that part of the inner ear related to balance. Experimenting with the notion of space gone awry, he insinuates a gently, inconspicuously dynamic perspective into the interior by scattering angled surfaces throughout. In the rear, a splinter of ceiling incised with a strip of light shears downward and runs along the centre of a long, narrow table in the middle of the dining room.

'We wanted a simple yet dynamic centrepiece that also had a function – in this case, a light – to hang over the communal table,' explains Askins. 'When you are standing, it divides the space. But when you sit, the space opens up.' Some things skew off the horizontal plane, others off the ground plane. In the rear, two columns that should provide a measure of verticality lean into each other instead. Since the ceilings are low and the restaurant is small, the designers could not tilt all the walls, as they would have wished, so they chose the ones that would have the greatest visual impact while still rendering the space usable. These slightly off-kilter elements – almost rhomboid mirrors that are not quite rectangular and not quite horizontal, veering walls with incisions that refuse to run parallel or perpendicular to the floor – set the gaze wandering drunkenly through the room, while the mind wonders what is off or whether the barman should cut us off. Together, the table flanked with benches, the line of light above (penetrating a hot-pink wall at the rear that lines a corridor leading to the kitchen) and the uneven mirrors form a disjointed, wholly un-ballasted cross at the back of the restaurant, echoing one of Rashid's typographical creations, a utopian hieroglyphic that evokes smiley faces more than words or cohesive ideas. 'Once we knew we wanted to play with planes and skewed shapes, we let the flow of the space and views help drive the lines,' says Askins.

Among the angles, Rashid has left his signature on this riotous canvas. Looking to the right upon entering, one sees, above a long line of small tables, an amorphous, glass-filled cut in the wall that is shaped something like the sound bubbles – Kapow! Kablam! Kaboom! – so typical of superhero comic books.

48

Designer:	Project:	Location:	Year of completion
Karim Rashid	Askew	New York, USA	2005

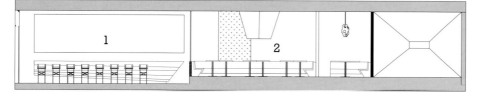

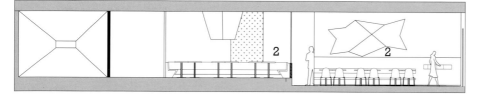

Preceding spread: In the rear, a sliver of ceiling is incised with
a strip of light. Certain elements skew off the horizontal plane,
others off the ground plane. Slightly off-kilter elements include
a long mirror that is not quite rectangular and not quite horizontal,
and columns that tilt in drunken confusion.

Section
1 Bar
2 Dining area

52

54

Architect:
Ippolito Fleitz Group

Project:
Trattoria da Loretta

Location:
Stuttgart, Germany

Year of completion:

Architect: Ippolito Fleitz Group
Project: Trattoria da Loretta
Location: Stuttgart, Germany

Text by Anneke Bokern
Photography by Zooey Braun

'Persistent lunching' is what got Ippolito Fleitz the commission for Trattoria da Loretta. 'Loretta Petti, who owns the Trattoria, is well known around Stuttgart, not only for her warm-hearted, Italian openness, but also for her cookery skills,' says Peter Ippolito. 'She used to run two delicatessens with catering, which served the most delicious dishes. We were regular customers.' Peter Ippolito and Gunter Fleitz, principals of the Ippolito Fleitz Group, may also have found favour with Petti by presenting themselves (also on their website) as 'identity architects'. For identity is the great leitmotif running through the interior design of Trattoria. It was Loretta Petti's childhood dream to open her own trattoria, a restaurant specializing in authentic Italian cuisine. She eventually found the ideal space on Büchsenstraße, close to Stuttgart's better nightclubs. She wanted a restaurant with a rustic Italian feel that would merge with this cool, hip area and be a fitting platform for her charismatic personality as hostess. No easy job. 'To start with, Loretta wanted the interior to look like a traditional Tuscan trattoria, a request that sent shivers down our spines,' says Ippolito. 'During one lively discussion, Loretta said, "Peter, deconstruct Tuscany for me, and put it back together in an original way." And that's exactly what we did.'

They set out to create the feel of Tuscany, while avoiding stereotypes. 'Loretta was with us every step of the way. We talked a lot.' Even so, says Ippolito, she was surprised when she saw the final result. No wonder, for the architects had taken nostalgic elements of her native land, fractured those ingredients and reformulated them in a highly ironic, unconventional way within an interior that is entirely fresh and up to date. Touristy clichés such as terracotta walls and statues of David were ruled out in favour of references for the in-crowd, such as 'Quant'è bella giovanezza', a poem by Renaissance prince Lorenzo II Magnifico that Italian schoolchildren learn by heart. Fragments of the poem written on the walls enter the diner's consciousness like snatches of a hip-hop song.

Opposite: Old-fashioned furnishings freshly interpreted. Sharing the ceiling are purpose-made chandeliers crafted from wire and copper-coloured paintings of enlarged doilies.

Above: The wallpaper is a collage of material motifs – wood grain, brocade, woven fabric – which, when combined with a mirrored strip, produce a number of optical illusions.

The 85-m² space – with its nooks and crannies and projecting volumes – is immersed in the deliciously creamy colours of tiramisu and nougat. In the entrance area, Ippolito and Fleitz installed a 2.5-m-high ceiling, just high enough to satisfy the legal requirements. 'It makes the rest of the restaurant look higher and more spacious,' says Ippolito. Grooves in the ceiling, into which lamps have been set, divide the interior into an entranceway, a dining area, a bar with seating and a stand-up bar.

Diners sit at one of three solid-wood tables, each of which accommodates up to 20 people, and take their cutlery and serviettes from drawers in the table. Surrounding the table at the rear of the L-shaped room are Tuscan chairs with wickerwork seats. Long benches line both sides of the other two tables. Apart from the Tuscan

chairs, the architects designed all furnishings at Trattoria, including the lamps with cylindrical woven-metal shades that hang above the tables. The atmosphere wraps customers in a warm blanket filled with the sight and smell and taste of 'Mama's home cooking'. Guests are invited to help themselves to drink. A large window behind the bar, which looks onto the kitchen, provides a view of the hostess and her team as they prepare the food.

The most striking design element at Trattoria da Loretta is the wallpaper, a collage of horizontal strips of varying widths that the architects developed together with textile designer Monika Trenkler. 'When it feels right, we like to work with artists and other designers,' says Ippolito. 'The idea for the wallpaper collage came to us quite early on in the design process.'

56

Architect:	Project:	Location:	Year of completion:
Ippolito Fleitz Group	Trattoria da Loretta	Stuttgart, Germany	2004

Opposite left: Fragments of 'Quant'è bella giovanezza',
an ode to youth by Renaissance prince Lorenzo Il Magnifico,
are written on the walls of the restaurant.

Opposite right: Lamps set into grooves in the ceiling
accentuate the shape of bar and counter, while defining this
area of the restaurant.
This page: Rustic walnut benches and tables are a foil for
the lush walls and slender shadows cast by ceiling lamps.

The Tuscan-remix concept has been applied to the walls in alternating bands of bright blue brocade, beige fabric, futuristic silver wallpaper and digitally printed wood grain. Few designs could be further removed from the modernist motto 'Less Is More'. What Ippolito and Fleitz had in mind were 'images of cosy rooms created in a contemporary way' with the richness needed to match Loretta's mouthwatering pannacotta.

The remix continues in the house-style of the graphics, another contribution by the Ippolito Fleitz Group. The logo, in elegant cursive lettering, appears on the façade in thin strokes of neon, which hark back to neon signs of the 1950s, a decade marked by a German yearning for all things Italian. Tuscany is visible in the fine stone floors and in the part contemporary, part conventional floral designs on a backlit window, the menu and the radiator covers. On the restaurant ceiling, forming the cream atop this delectable Italian dessert, are computer-scanned lace doilies, which have been enlarged and painted with copper-coloured hammertone enamel. Mama goes modern –
but not without a hint of handicraft.

THE ARCHITECTS HAVE TAKEN NOSTALGIC ELEMENTS OF TUSCANY, FRACTURED THOSE INGREDIENTS AND REFORMULATED THEM.

Architect:	Project:	Location:	Year of completion:
Ippolito Fleitz Group	Trattoria da Loretta	Stuttgart, Germany	2004

59

Floor plan
1 Dining area
2 Bar
3 Kitchen
4 Cloak room
5 Lavatories

A mix of patterns in shades of nougat: textile artist Monika Trenkler designed the walls.

62

64

Architect:
Jason Caroline Design

Project:
Kushiyaki

Location:
Hong Kong, China

Year of completion:
2005

Architect: Jason Caroline Design
Project: Kushiyaki
Location: Hong Kong, China

Text by Masaaki Takahashi
Photography by John Butlin

Created as part of an urban-redevelopment project for pop-culture epicentre Mong Kok, Langham Place soars above the modest skyline of this old inner-city district on Hong Kong's Kowloon Peninsula. The 15-storey shopping mall arrived on the scene in 2004, transforming its surroundings into a futuristic cityscape straight out of Blade Runner. Linking the twin towers of the hotel and office volumes of the complex, the building (measuring over 167,000 m^2) has markedly high-tech, science-fiction elements running through its design, strongly characterizing both the interior and exterior of the structure. Inside, visitors encounter images of the mall's mascot, a beautiful girl drawn in the style of Japanese anime, who smiles down enticingly from various points in the towering space. Kushiyaki, the first in a proposed chain of Japanese restaurants, can be found on the twelfth storey.

The three responsible for the interior design are Jason Yung, Caroline Ma and Keith Chan of Jason Caroline Design. To craft a snapshot-like image of Japan – an illusion of a Japanese landscape that would be familiar to Hong Kong residents – they used texture, colour, ornament and an intimate sense of scale. Taking graphic art as a starting point, the designers came up with a logo for the restaurant before turning their attention to tinted mirrors for the walls.

Preceding spread and opposite: Picnic-style tables feature tops of stonewashed oak. Patterned glass panels evoke images of oriental tattoos.

Left and right: Three Japanese fabrics were chosen for the chairs at Kushiyaki.

Here, they manipulated a standard chrysanthemum pattern into a motif that has come to symbolize the restaurant. Elsewhere, they integrated contemporary design principles into the space as a contrast to the more traditional Japanese references.

With a dining area measuring a mere 230 m², Kushiyaki is on the small side, and it was important to maintain a balance between fostering an elegant ambience and fitting in as much seating as possible – conditions as familiar to Tokyo designers as to their counterparts in Hong Kong. Three 4.5-m-long picnic-style tables, capable of seating a total of 48 diners, dominate the main restaurant area. In addition to this bench seating, the tiny space also offers six chairs at the bar, seven stand-alone tables and a VIP room, complete with tatami, that can cater for parties of up to ten people.

All furniture has been custom-made on a scale slightly smaller than usual to reflect the Japanese origins of the design.

Each space and seating type features a different texture, with purple wave-patterned fabric used for the wall panels and three Japanese fabrics for the dining chairs. Slate flooring in the entrance area makes an interesting contrast to tatami in the VIP room, as does the stonewashed oak of the picnic-style tabletops to the walnut veneer of the seating. A variety of elements employed to define certain spaces include patterned frosted mirrors in the open kitchen, a series of hanging lamps in the main dining hall and, in the VIP room, lengths of twisted rope combined with surfaces of mirrored stainless steel. The people of Hong Kong have long taken an interest in Japanese culture, incorporating it into their own cultural mix since the 1980s.

66

Architect:	Project:	Location:	Year of completion:
Jason Caroline Design	Kushiyaki	Hong Kong, China	2005

Opposite left: Purple wave-patterned fabric has been used for wall panels.
Opposite right: Lengths of twisted rope give the VIP room a sense of privacy.

Above: Patterned frosted glass panels were used to define the open kitchen.

TV programmes, manga, furniture and other aspects of the Japanese lifestyle have all had an influence on life in Hong Kong. The island represents the world's largest market for Japanese cuisine, and Japanese restaurants within the city number around 900.

Taking into account the population of Hong Kong, which has just over seven million inhabitants, no-one can deny that 'eating Japanese' has permeated the Hong Kong way of life. A visit to any supermarket will reveal Japanese delicacies displayed in the same way as local foodstuffs rather than being tucked away in the foreign-food section. It's easy to see that this hunger for things Japanese is not just a passing fad, but part of a practice firmly entrenched in the lifestyle of countless Hong Kong residents. Despite a menu filled with relatively expensive choices, Japanese restaurants show no sign of losing their popularity, a phenomenon that can be explained by the attachment of a certain status to those who frequent such establishments.

The eating habits of Hong Kongers prove that the world of cuisine is a world without borders. When choosing a spot for the ideal date, members of the younger generation are apt to select a kaiten zushi restaurant, where plates of sushi circulate on conveyor belts past waiting diners.
A Hong Kong market with a keen eye on Japan is experiencing a boom of restaurants that are serving up cutting-edge design as a backdrop to mouth-watering menus. And Hong Kong firms are creating innovative décors, many of which surpass even those in Tokyo, a city where designers have long felt the heat from a demanding clientele that seems to expect retail and restaurant interiors to change with the seasons.

TO CRAFT A SNAPSHOT-LIKE IMAGE OF JAPAN THE TEAM AT JASON CAROLINE DESIGN USED TEXTURE, COLOUR, ORNAMENT AND AN INTIMATE SENSE OF SCALE.

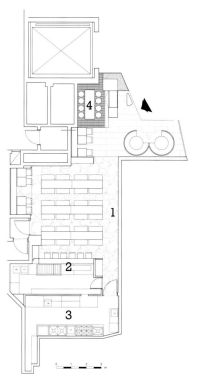

Architect:
Jason Caroline Design

Project:
Kushiyaki

Location:
Hong Kong, China

Year of completion:
2005

69

Floor plan
1 Dining area
2 Bar
3 Kitchen
4 VIP room

Bench seating has been
finished in walnut veneer.

HOMEM
CROQU
FILLED
WITH
CHEESE
SPINAC
SHRIMF

ADE
TIES

THER
AND
HOR

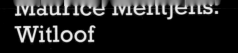

74

Architect: Project: Location: Year of completion:
Maurice Mentjens   Witloof   Maastricht, Netherlands   2005

Architect: Maurice Mentjens
Project: Witloof
Location: Maastricht, Netherlands

Text by Anneke Bokern
Photography by Arjen Schmitz

Witloof, the name of a restaurant in Maastricht, the Netherlands, is programmatic. Witloof is the Flemish word for 'Belgian endive' or 'chicory'. Legend has it that a 19th-century Belgian farmer accidentally discovered its culinary qualities. True or not, witloof, which plainly has its roots in Belgium, is a perfect name for a restaurant specializing in Belgian food.

At Witloof, Belgium influences not only the cuisine but also the interior design of the restaurant, the work of Limburg-based Maurice Mentjens. In the eyes of many, Belgium lacks a distinctive image and does not immediately suggest a particular style of interior design. For that reason, when Mentjens was asked to do the interior, he 'made a short trip to Belgium with the restaurant's owner-to-be. We spent a couple of evenings trawling the pubs of Antwerp and Ghent to get an idea of the typical Belgian interior design.' Their conclusion: the style of Belgian interior design is no style. The interiors they saw featured a conglomeration of stylistic elements, often assembled without rhyme or reason. Many of the pubs seemed to be the work of do-it-yourself enthusiasts who had gradually patched them together. This matched the slightly schizophrenic ideas of Mentjens' client.

Opposite: An array of vintage picture frames hanging behind the bar display old vases, along with the usual glasses, bottles and old teapots needed for operating a bar.

Left: A mix of styles in a confined space. The 'chip shop' leads rather unexpectedly to a formal drawing room.
Right: Mentjens combined green-gold brocade wallpaper with simple, rustic IKEA chairs and Art-Deco plates from the flea market.

He wanted a highly convivial atmosphere within a hip environment enhanced by a generous dose of kitsch. Accordingly, the designer divided the space into three areas inspired by three Belgian clichés.

The wood-panelled entrance zone, with its simple wooden furniture, was inspired by the image of a cabin in the Ardennes. The smooth parquet surfaces are not particularly rustic, however, and combined with the black wall to the right of the entrance and the ornate brass chandelier, they generate a trendy urban yet cosily relaxed ambience.

The division between the entrance zone and the tiled section is marked by a strip of red neon. Red symbolizes the border between Flanders and Wallonia, which divides Dutch-speaking and French-speaking Belgians, while also alluding to the neon lighting of Belgian brothels. One wall displays a yellow neon and black wall - represent the Belgian flag. The same shades repeated in the toilets, where black doors with heart-shaped peepholes reveal a red space and yellow space.

The symbolism does not end there. Belgium also features a striking division between urban and rural areas, and the neon strips separate the 'country cabin' section of the restaurant from the adjoining 'big city' section. The wood-panelled entrance zone lends access to a space tiled in white, including the bar found here. Intended as a cool, urban environment, this fashionably minimal dining room has aesthetic roots tied to the pragmatic interiors of Belgian chip shops, which have a trend-conscious aspect all their own. For the Belgian frituur (Dutch) or friterie (French) cannot be dismissed as a spare, sparse cubicle. Such shops are sacrosanct to the Belgians. Nothing at Witloof is spare or sparse. Mentjens has covered the wall behind the bar with old-fashioned wallpaper, a nice contrast to the tiled surfaces. Mounted to the wall as shelving for bottles are glass showcases featuring gold-painted, pseudo-antique picture frames.

Architect:
Maurice Mentjens

Project:
Witloof

Location:
Maastricht, Netherlands

Year of completion:
2005

77

Opposite top: Oak panelling in the entrance area evokes the image of a simple cabin in the Ardennes. The statue of Manneken Pis provides an unmistakably Belgian touch. Opposite bottom: Chandeliers from a flea market in Tongeren add warmth to the white-tiled bar.

This page: A 'Gothic' cellar features Castelo tiles whose beige and black motif is repeated on the walls. Untreated wooden tables and chairs form a leitmotif throughout the restaurant.

78

Architect:
Maurice Mentjens

Project:
Witloof

Location:
Maastricht, Netherlands

Year of completion:
2005

The black backdrop and dramatic built-in lighting make the schnapps bottles sparkle, their warm colours forming a rich counterbalance to the ascetic white tiles.

Green-gold wallpaper behind the bar transitions into the third section of the restaurant area – the 'Salon' – a space that resembles Grandma's reserved-for-Sunday-afternoon parlour. Here, Mentjens has taken chic kitsch to the extreme, decorating the walls of this Belgian drawing room with ornamental plates, golden cherubs and vintage 'ancestral' photographs mounted in heavy, ornate frames.

A staircase with a wrought-iron banister spirals from the Salon to the basement, an underground space dating from the late Middle Ages. Mentjens immersed this dining room in a Gothic atmosphere. Flooring features black tiles with a bright-beige floral motif, inspired by neogothic designs. The motif is repeated on the walls and on the vaulted ceiling, where the shiny black curlicues and interlocked circles stand out against a matte-black ground. A sprinkling of little red lights adorns one projecting wall, and a black chandelier hangs in the middle of the room. But the pièce de resistance is the black bar, which in this cryptal space could be an altar, a shrine to St Schnapps. The bar is a fitting reference to the cliché that Belgian Catholicism embraces all of life's pleasures. Few restaurant interiors could be further removed from the austerity of modernism. Mentjens has housed four distinctive interiors within an 80-m² space in which opposites clash and only the simple tables and chairs made of untreated wood provide a central theme. But the whole thing hangs together in an inexplicable way, rather like Belgium itself – a multilingual, individualistic country that lacks an image.

'WE SPENT A COUPLE OF EVEN-INGS TRAWLING THE PUBS OF ANTWERP AND GHENT TO GET AN IDEA OF THE TYPICAL BELGIAN INTERIOR DESIGN.'

Maurice Mentjens

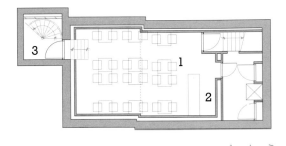

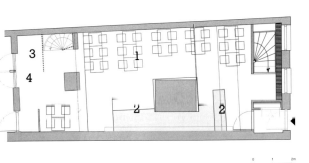

Floor plan
1 Dining area
2 Bar
3 Cloak room
4 Lavatories

Opposite: Where cosiness and coolness meet. The tiny sansevieria plants seen on the wall to the left are found in many Belgian interiors.

Torii Design Office:
Hitsuji

84

Architect: Project: Location: Year of completion:
Torii Design Office   Hitsuji   Nagoya, Japan   2005

Architect: Torii Design Office
Project: Hitsuji
Location: Nagoya, Japan

Text by Masaaki Takahashi
Photography by Nacása & Partners Inc

Located in Tenpaku-ku, Nagoya City – where it counts among its neighbours a number of large-scale cooperatives, condos, a sports facility, a huge park and a theatre – the Hitsuji restaurant targets local residents, particularly young families, as well as visitors to the area. The speciality of the restaurant is jinngisukann, a dish of barbecued mutton and vegetables prepared at the table in a vessel that looks like the helmet of an ancient Mongolian soldier.

Nagoya-based Yoshinori Torii, who created the interior in collaboration with Type A/B, is a veteran of restaurant design. He approached the project by inventing a mascot for the restaurant, a little girl name Hitsuji (Japanese for 'sheep'). Local illustrator and colourist Chie Hikita put his ideas on paper, and the child was born. Torii believed that associating mutton with an appealing figure like Hitsuji would improve the image of a meat that has not been very popular in most of Japan.

The interior, with its monochrome colour scheme, radiates the dreamlike world of an imaginative child. By painting private areas dark, the dining arca light, and the entrance zone a shade in between the two, Torii has managed to silhouette both diners and cuisine.

Preceding spread: Monochrome images of sheep surround the dining area.
Opposite: Chairs and stools are made from aluminium.

Left: A style that is part high-tech and part vernacular permeates the interior of the restaurant.
Right: Hitsuji, the cartoon 'mascot' who gives the restaurant its name, was created to improve the image of lamb and mutton, foods that have never been particularly popular in Japan.

Monochrome photographs of a flock of sheep, which are printed on graphic sheets, have been mounted high on the walls as if to emphasize the height of the ceiling. Torii intentionally opted for low-resolution photography to give the flock a rather blurred, impressionistic appearance, as in a dream.

Further pursuing his ambition to change the general Japanese aversion to mutton, Torii kept the design of the interior simple, injecting a kind of 'cool café' ambience into Hitsuji. He can be encouraged in his efforts by the realization that eating raw fish, which people all over the world now know (and love) as sushi, would have been unthinkable in the West in the not-too-distant past. Whereas lamb occasionally appears in dishes served at foreign-style restaurants in Japan, until recently diners looking for mutton have had to

visit the country's Indian eateries or journey to Hokkaido in northern Japan, where jinngisukann is part of the regional cuisine. Today they can also join the growing number of people who are enjoying the dish throughout the country, even in Tokyo. Part of the rise in popularity is due to a fear of BSE (mad cow disease), which is linked to eating beef. Although barbecued mutton may be an acquired taste, Torii believes that those who try it will come back to Hitsuji again and again.

An increase in the appreciation of unfamiliar dishes goes hand in hand with a huge upsurge in the amount of restaurants in Japan. As interior designers convert one space after another into a plethora of places where people can eat out, the search for something special – that exceptional restaurant which offers not only good food but also a truly unique environment – is becoming an exciting game to many diners.

Architect:	Project:	Location:	Year of completion:
Torii Design Office	Hitsuji	Nagoya, Japan	2005

87

Opposite left: Staff members wear T-shirts printed with the image of an appealing little girl named Hitsuji.
Opposite right: A room in which guests sit on the floor features carpeting that covers not only the floor, but also walls and ceiling.

Above: Counter and tabletops are finished in melamine.

88

Architect:
Torii Design Office

Project:
Hitsuji

Location:
Nagoya, Japan

Year of completion:
2005

The designer who wants to stay ahead of this game, or at least to match the moves of the best players, has to put a great deal of thought into what pleases the clientele. His or her interior design should make people feel relaxed and happy, while also contributing to a smoothly running operation and conveying an interesting concept.

Torii likes to create a good balance among interior, service and food. He focuses on a comfortable setting that allows staff members, including those in the kitchen, to perform their duties with obvious pleasure.

A key element in every design is an uninterrupted circulation route, particularly for employees, whose 'smiles turn diners into regular customers', according to Torii. Staff members at the Torii Design Office are required to spend their first year working part-time in a restaurant, where they learn what goes into producing such smiles. On-site experience is vital if they are to design restaurants, explains the architect. They come back to the office with a good understanding of how a restaurant and its personnel function – and with enthusiastic ideas about how to develop even better spaces for participants in the game of 'spot the perfect restaurant'.

'A KEY ELEMENT IN EVERY DESIGN IS AN UNINTERRUPTED CIRCULATION ROUTE, PARTICULARLY FOR EMPLOYEES, WHOSE "SMILES TURN DINERS INTO REGULAR CUSTOMERS."'

Yoshinori Torii

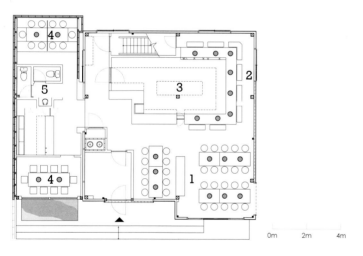

Floor plan
1 Dining area
2 Bar
3 Kitchen
4 Private room
5 Lavatories

Opposite: Pendant lamps emphasize the height of the interior.

OQO
Most served dish:

CLASS STEAN PRAW DUMP

Hawkins\Brown: OQO

Architect:	Project:	Location:	Year of completion:
Hawkins\Brown	OQO	London, England	2004

Architect: Hawkins\Brown
Project: OQO
Location: London, England

Text by Sarah Martín Pearson
Photography by Simon Phipps

Take prize-winning Chinese restaurateur Mark Chan, founder of ECapital Shanghai restaurant and nominee for the Carlton TV 2003 London Oriental Restaurant of the Year award; architect Jeremy Walker of Hawkins\Brown; and graphic designer John Simpson of SEA Design. Put the three in a cocktail shaker and prepare to enjoy a long, cool OQO. Following the latest trend in London eateries, this tapas and cocktail bar with an oriental twist serves up an enticing menu of contemporary Chinese food with European influences accompanied by cocktails ranging from the classics to imaginative in-house creations. Situated on London's leafy Islington Green, OQO is reputed to have a mantra that goes, 'Thou shalt not eat without cocktails; thou shalt not drink without Chinese tapas.'

At their first professional gathering – not counting a night out at the cinema, followed by a few beers – Chan, Walker and Simpson came up with OQO, a moniker that's fun to visualize and a puzzler to pronounce. The next step was to develop a brand identity geared to the new restaurant concept. As for the interior itself, the circular forms of the logo combined with the characteristic linearity of projects by Hawkins\Brown add up to a space that unites the organic, in terms of materials, with the minimal, in terms of furnishings, for an overall ambience in which lighting and graphics are key.

Preceding spread: Opposite the bar are immense images of exotic food.
Opposite: The main entrance is framed in a black, L-shaped archway whose surface provides a backdrop for illuminated logos outlined in white. Passers-by have an excellent view of the interior through large windows facing the street.

Left: The front of the bar, with its built-in lighting, is clad in a back-lit glass and wood laminate, which adds a touch of nature to the interior.
Right: White, wall-mounted light boxes wrap around a corner of the dining room, suggesting volume. An untreated wall in raw brown concrete features grooves that evoke the raked sands of a Zen garden.

The main entrance overlooks the street through large windows. Inside, the most striking component is a 14-m-long bar that extends the entire length of the space. Built-in lighting glows through a timber veneer held by layers of illuminated glass in the bar front. Lining the bar are stools with translucent seats which pick-up light from the bar. The end of the bar encloses an open-plan kitchen, where working chefs occasionally raise their heads to greet customers. Reflected in the black-granite counter are halo-like images that adorn the wall behind the bar, an unexpected result of two things: a manufacturing mix-up and the decision to halve the bird's-eye-view photographs of cocktails. 'The images were so strong that we cut them in half and arranged them in semicircles behind the bar,' says Walker. 'And we ordered a matte granite bar top, but a polished one was delivered instead.' Completing the graphic intervention are columns opposite the bar, which sport blow-ups of exotic food, and menus and match-boxes bearing the same images.

Other light sources include a row of small bare bulbs suspended over the bar and white, wall-mounted light boxes that warm the dining room with a diffused, fluorescent glow. Certain spots feature a cluster of light boxes, while other boxes wrap around corners, suggesting volume, or lead guests down the stairs to a dining area in the basement. A play of light and transparency in the toilets reveals the shadows of occupants on translucent polycarbonate-panelled walls suffused in pink light from a strip of LEDs. 'We planned for shadows in this area,' says Walker. 'However, when we inspected the polycarbonate walls, they looked almost transparent.' Asked in advance whether the restaurant was going to have 'see-through toilets', he replied, 'Not quite. We shall see.' Walker explains that, like the cuisine, 'the interiors rely on experimental playfulness with materials to conjure something fresh and new'. Much of the design was improvised on site, often as a result of fortuitous events that gradually helped shape the space.

Architect:	Project:	Location:	Year of completion:
Hawkins\Brown	OQO	London, England	2004

Opposite top: The end of the bar encloses an open-plan kitchen, where working chefs occasionally raise their heads to greet customers. The restaurant serves a variety of creative Chinese tapas with a European flavour.

Above: Bird's-eye-view photographs of cocktail glasses have been cut in half and used to decorate the wall behind the bar. Their halo-like images are reflected in the polished black-granite counter, completing the pictures while also suggesting the OQO logo.

Architect:
Hawkins\Brown

Project:
OQO

Location:
London, England

Year of completion:
2004

As Chan said before the opening in December 2004, 'Accidents can be the most beautiful things, and I look forward to them happening.'

The lighting scheme is based on a dimly illuminated space enhanced by a play of light. Most elements are kept in half shadow or, thanks to built-in lighting, serve as light sources themselves. Continuous black concrete flooring blends with dark walls and ceilings, and illuminated, white-outlined logos stand out against the surface of the black L-shaped archway framing the main entrance. An untreated wall in raw brown concrete is perhaps the only eye-catching architectural feature that emerges from the darkness. Parallel grooves in this wall resemble the raked sands of a Zen garden. Moveable furniture corresponds to Chan's preference for a flexible space that adapts easily to the needs of customers. Tables and chairs line the perimeter of the ground-floor dining room, while a chill-out zone in the middle of the space offers the comfort of two black leather-upholstered sofas, combined with ottomans and small cubic tables in white. This ensemble, which is visible from the street, attracts passers-by and adds extra breathing space and a sense of exclusivity to the room.

At OQO, a spatial design merges successfully with the introduction of a new brand image. Architect and graphic designer collaborated to satisfy all points of the client's brief: an environment crafted by lighting, simplicity and flexibility and distinguished by the seamless integration of architecture, graphics and photography.

'ACCIDENTS CAN BE THE MOST BEAUTIFUL THINGS, AND I LOOK FORWARD TO THEM HAPPENING.'
Mark Chan

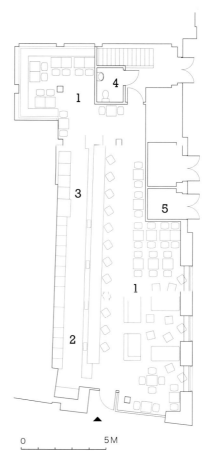

0   5 M

Floor plan
1 Dining area
2 Bar
3 Kitchen
4 Lavatory
5 Storage

Opposite: The fun of experimenting with materials led the designers to enclose the toilets in translucent polycarbonate-panelled walls suffused in pink light from a strip of LEDs. As a result, the shadows of occupants can be seen by those on the other side of these walls.

Glass
Most served dish:

Andrea Lupacchini Architect:
Glass

103

104

Architect:	Project:	Location:	Year of completion:
Andrea Lupacchini Architect	Glass	Rome, Italy	2005

Architect: Andrea Lupacchini Architect
Project: Glass
Location: Rome, Italy

Text by Monica Zerboni
Photography by Beatrice Pediconi

Is there a secret recipe for transforming an average eatery into a popular restaurant? Essential to the success of a restaurant are four basic ingredients: a first-class location, a pleasant atmosphere, a select clientele and, of course, a mouthwatering menu. Each of the four seems a perfect match for the elements that make up Glass, a Roman restaurant that has thrived from day one.

Young architect Andrea Lupacchini found himself faced with a difficult task. He was asked to convert the interior of an existing building on Vicolo del Cinque in Trastevere – a highly traditional and touristy area of Rome with quintessentially historical features – into a trendy restaurant and wine bar that would feature local cuisine. During the summer, the open windows of residential buildings along this narrow lane reveal coffered ceilings and exposed beams. The façades of these buildings display an abundance of natural stone – travertine and basalt, in most cases – well worn by years of gradual deterioration.

Lupacchini reports that the client, who owns another restaurant in the city, asked for 'a sophisticated ambience that would reflect the high quality of the food to be served': Italian cuisine made from traditional ingredients, but prepared in an innovative style.

Preceding spread: In the middle of the room is a vertical screen made of steel and satin-finished glass that features (on opposite sides) a work of art and the logo of the restaurant.
Opposite: The steps of the sculptural staircase are irregularly shaped, acid-aged steel boxes with built-in reinforcement. The angular handrail, which follows the meandering shape of the staircase, comprises three sections of tubular steel.

Left: The use of peperino stone for the bar counter (right) is a tribute to traditional Roman architecture.
Right: Rest-room walls and floors are clad in 60-x-60-cm tiles with a coarse grey texture. Doors are made from acid-aged steel sheet. Elliptical designer basins boast slender taps.

'To achieve this goal, we used materials belonging to Rome's urban tradition and adapted them to a modern, fashionable context.' Indeed, the space is full of innovative solutions that proudly coexist with the architectural heritage of Rome.

The restaurant is divided into three sections: dining room, kitchen, and a space accommodating toilets and cloakroom. The dining area is split into two levels that are connected by a sculptural staircase: an autonomous structure of acid-aged steel that pairs irregularly shaped steps and whimsically angular handrails.

Highlighting the bright, shiny dining room is a slender screen, 4.5 m tall, made of steel and satin-finished glass. Displaying a work of art on the side facing the diners and the logo of the

restaurant on the side facing the street, this striking 'megalith' – a towering material homage to the name of the restaurant – catches the eye of passers-by. Further enhancing the impact made by this room are columns still displaying the building's original, 17th-century masonry and ancient wooden beams overhead. Built flush into the wengé flooring are long, glass-panelled cases. Inside each illuminated case, resting on a bed of quarry stones, are bottles of vintage wine and other food-related items.

The tall steel-and-glass megalith is not the only artistic element on display. Covering part of the walls are gleaming steel panels that artist Marco Filippetti has used as canvasses for his creations: works of art crafted with blue pigments, acid, coloured wax and resins.

106

Architect:
Andrea Lupacchini Architect

Project:
Glass

Location:
Rome, Italy

Year of completion:
2005

107

Opposite left: Stainless-steel cylinders in various sizes hang at staggered heights, invading the space and providing direct light to the tables below, as well as diffuse light emitted from horizontal slits in the tubing.

Opposite right: Built flush into the wenge flooring are long, glass-panelled cases. Inside each illuminated case, resting on a bed of quarry stones, are bottles of vintage wine and other food-related items.

This page: Walls in the dining room feature steel panels that bear the creative marks of artist Marco Filippetti, who has scarred these surfaces with acid, blue pigments, iron oxide, wax and coloured resins.

108

Architect:
Andrea Lupacchini Architect

Project:
Glass

Location:
Rome, Italy

Year of completion:
2005

One might say that Filippetti has scarred the polished surface, leaving it marked by the wounds of his intervention. Horizontal light boxes set into the walls at eye level encompass much of the dining room, where the architect has made a distinction between the wall proper and the partially exposed steel panelling behind it.

Centrally positioned in the restaurant area is the bar, a trapezial block wrapped in bands of peperino and basalt. Lupacchini points out that the use of peperino was a deliberate choice, because at one end of the bar the counter becomes part of the staircase. The two elements make a harmonious entity, thanks largely to the presence of this particular stone.

All things considered, however, the focal point of the project is light, which the architects treated as a vital architectural element, a tangible addition to the realization of an extraordinary environment. Sunshine rarely finds its way into the narrow, densely developed, cobbled lane. At Glass, the only natural light entering the dining area comes through the floor-to-ceiling glass door at the entrance. During opening hours, a system based on PLC (programmable logic control) technology dims and intensifies illumination – both direct and indirect light sources – throughout the restaurant. This lighting system, which encircles the perimeter of the room, plays up the contrast between the two surfaces mentioned earlier: the wall and the steel surface behind it. Beams of light run rhythmically from the top to the bottom of openings in the wall that reveal glimpses of the metal backdrop. Overhead is a forest of stainless-steel cylinders, which hang from the ceiling at different heights. Dominating the space, these lamps emit a direct flow of light to the tables below, while also spreading diffuse lighting from staccato horizontal incisions made in their tubular fittings. Everywhere one looks, light dances through the interior, from bar counter to logo to stairway to works of art.

'TO CREATE AN INTERIOR THAT WOULD REFLECT THE QUALITY OF THE FOOD TO BE SERVED, WE USED MATERIALS BELONGING TO ROME'S URBAN TRADITION.'

Andrea Lupacchini

Opposite: The focal point of the project is light, which the architect treated as an architectural element. Throughout the interior – from designer tables and glazed floor cases to wall niches and works of art – light plays a starring role.

TUNA-BA-
TUNA STE
GRILLED
GARLICAN
WITH GR
BUTTER
AND CUCU
YOGHURT

A00 Architecture: a FuturePerfect

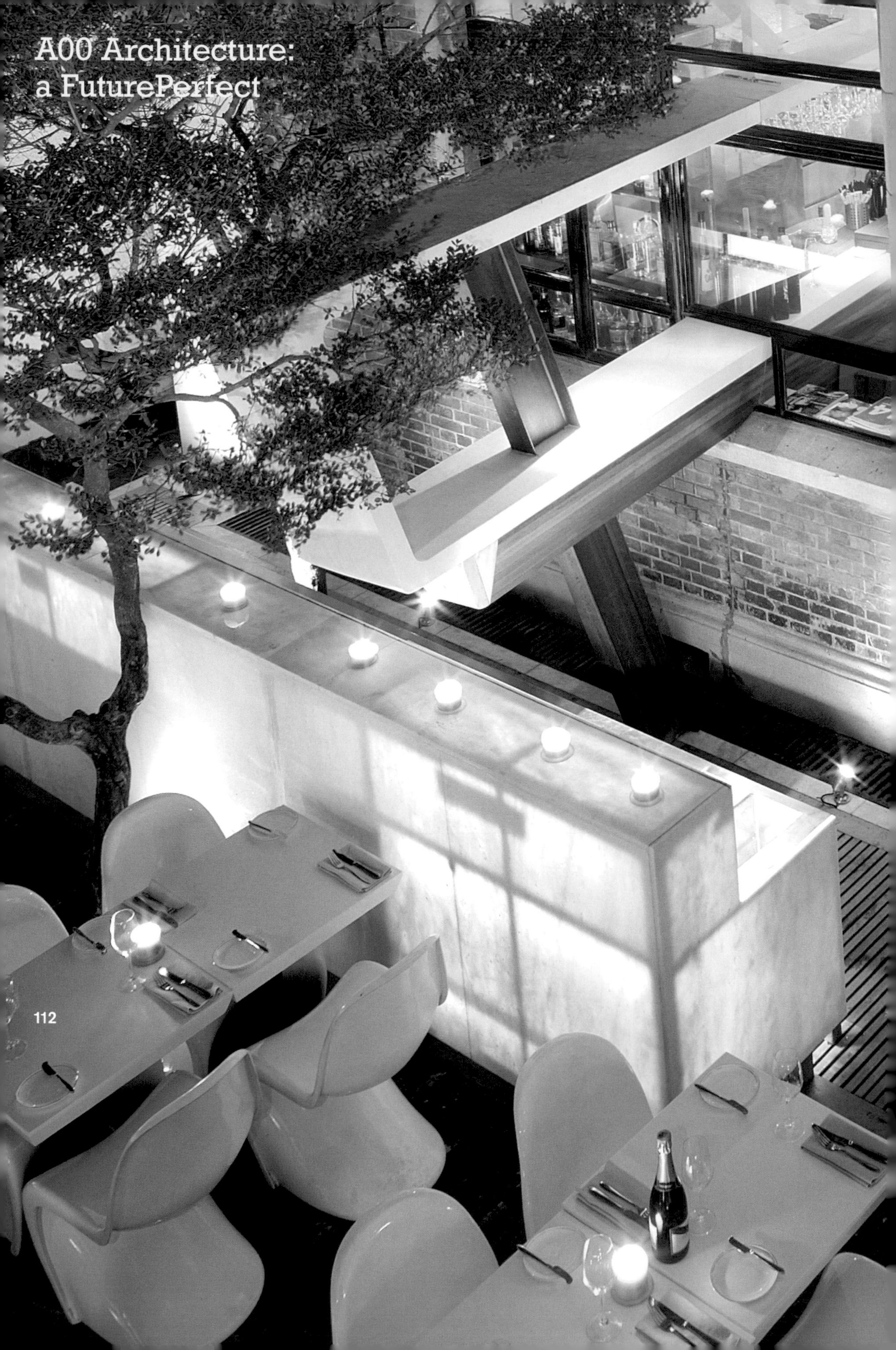

Architect:	Project:	Location:	Year of completion:
A00 Architecture	a FuturePerfect	Shanghai, China	2005

Architect: A00 Architecture
Project: a FuturePerfect
Location: Shanghai, China

Text by Carolien van Tilburg
Photography by But-Sou Lai, Gary Edwards
and Shenghui Photography Company

Located in a blind alley just off Huashanlu, in the trendy area of Shanghai, is a FuturePerfect, a restaurant adjacent to the historical Old House Inn. Leaving the dark lane, the visitor enters the bright, futuristic courtyard of the restaurant. Gleaming Panton dining chairs, an outdoor bar and shade trees: ideal for sultry summer evenings in Shanghai. When the weather turns cool, heating lanterns warm the terrace. The restaurant bar pierces a glass wall to penetrate the court-yard, making an architectonic statement while also offering extra work space during the summer season. Highlighting the compact, light-filled dining room inside are one colour and one material: lime green and corrugated cardboard, respectively. This is not an ordinary eatery. Devotees of design have been at work here.

Architecture firm A00 (A Zero Zero) was asked to distil from a hotchpotch of ideas a concept for a restaurant with courtyard. The main requirement was the colour green. 'As for the rest, it was all contradictory,' recalls Raefer K. Wallis of A00. 'The client, A.M. Therapy, is made up of three partners for whom we've done many separate projects in the past. The brief evolved informally, as part of quite a few brainstorming sessions. It was never formally written down.

Preceding spread and opposite: Piercing the wall of the restaurant is an acrylic-resin bar that serves as a linking pin between interior and exterior. The solid white volume is visibly supported by a steel column.

Left: The courtyard area of the bar enlarges the work space during the summer season.
Right: The logo pops up everywhere, including as a carved version on the concrete wall at the entrance.

On the one hand, the design had to be "never seen before" yet recognizable. It had to be stark and modern, yet warm and cosy. It had to be chic yet casual. A client wearing sneakers and a T-shirt needed to feel comfortable having a glass of wine with someone dressed in a suit. It had to accommodate kids and business executives.' As if all that wasn't enough, the architects were also asked to follow the precepts of feng shui. The entrance was to include the colour red, and a mountain landscape had to be incorporated into their design of the restaurant. 'In the end, what we chose to emphasize was the contradiction in all these words and ideas,' says Sacha Silva of the design team, adding that the aim was to 'architecturalize' the requirements and meet as many of them as possible.

Together with the SGTH graphic-design team, they opted for a fusion of features, with regard to the name of the restaurant, as well as to its architecture. The décor both inside and outside combines modern and traditional elements and new and used materials. The past lies sealed within the neighbouring boutique hotel and the old, weathered walls and materials of the courtyard. On the terrace, three rough-hewed stone columns, remnants of the old courtyard, represent a mountain scene. At the same time, however, the minimalist courtyard has the look of a contemporary space. Curvaceous white garden chairs stand out elegantly against their rough-walled surroundings. The concrete entrance complements warm wood flooring, which in turn contrasts with interior details in fresh lime green and crisp white. Plain corrugated-cardboard chairs are comfortably padded. Here a range of materials and colours unite in harmony to generate a clean, contemporary, chill-free atmosphere.

With great attention to detail, A00 furnished the space as efficiently as possible. By concealing the air-conditioning system, the architects were able to integrate two intimate window niches into the plan. Manoeuvring its way through the space, the bar forms a partition between two dining tables, and against the wall is a space-saving banquette.

116

Architect:	Project:	Location:	Year of completion:
A00 Architecture	a FuturePerfect	Shanghai, China	2005

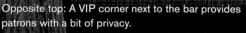

117

Opposite top: A VIP corner next to the bar provides patrons with a bit of privacy.
Opposite bottom: The architects aimed for a maximum use of floor space to seat customers. Graphic images cover wall and ceilings.

This page: A00 took advantage of the concealed air-conditioning system to create two semi-private window niches.

Architect:
A00 Architecture

Project:
a FuturePerfect

Location:
Shanghai, China

Year of completion:
2005

A so-called 'VIP table' features a recess for cooling a bottle of champagne or wine. The collaboration between graphic designers and architects is clearly visible. Embedded in each custom-designed table is a stainless-steel logo, and graphics found on menus and website are repeated on the walls of the restaurant.

A FuturePerfect can fit 56 guests into a space that is only 120 m². On evenings when all seats are taken, the room may feel a bit claustrophobic. Although A00 originally had a more spaciously arranged 'lounge' in mind, A.M. Therapy is well satisfied. 'The client was comfortable with packing in the guests. He thinks this invites impromptu chats with strangers at the next table. He's had the same experience at another successful restaurant, Arch,' says Silva. The approach seems to be working. Night after night, the restaurant is fully booked. A disadvantage of such enormous success, of course, is that only a few months after the restaurant opened, both upholstery and menus were already showing signs of age.

What's very clear is that a great deal of enthusiasm went into this project. Even the menu displays a quirky exuberance, with dishes like Buffalo Wings, Quack Quack and Apollo's Parcel. And what about raising a glass to the achievements of architects and designers with cocktails called A Zero Zero Shot and Sasha Silver? Perfection, after all, remains a thing of the future, so why not drink to the present? Cheers!

'ON THE ONE HAND, THE DESIGN HAD TO BE "NEVER SEEN BEFORE" YET RECOGNIZABLE. IT HAD TO BE STARK AND MODERN, YET WARM AND COSY. IT HAD TO BE CHIC YET CASUAL.'
Raefer K. Wallis

Opposite: Contrasting textures mark the interior. The raw look of corrugated-cardboard chairs is complemented by that of wooden tables with smoothly painted surfaces. The choice of fabrics also varies from coarse to cuddly.

Top left: Green is used throughout the interior.
Top right: Embedded in each custom-designed table is a stainless-steel logo.

ILLE,

ED

ITH

EESE

S

CELERY

EL

Claudio Colucci Design: Delicabar

122

124

Architect: Claudio Colucci Design
Project: Delicabar
Location: Paris, France

Text by Masaaki Takahashi
Photography by Francesca Mantovani

It's common knowledge that each bank of the River Seine boasts a unique ambience: the Right Bank, home to aristocrats and financiers, versus the Left Bank, the haunt of artists and intellectuals. Money dominates the rather conservative Rive Droite, while culture and the arts reign on the more bohemian Rive Gauche. The former stands for conservatism, and the latter champions a more liberal stance.

Delicabar, whose cutting-edge interior positions it at the forefront of design in the city, can be found in La Grande Epicerie de Paris, an annex of Bon Marché, the only department store situated firmly on the Left Bank. Inside La Grande Epicerie, an astounding diversity of gourmet foodstuffs awaits the customer. Here, every outlet vies for attention, attempting to overshadow its rivals with elegant packaging and a magnificent display. A must-see for any self-respecting gourmand, the store has such a wealth of delights to offer that it's easy to spend an entire day here with absolutely no sense of ennui. Above this haven of choice morsels, a floor replete with women's fashion accommodates the boutiques of such brands as Marc Jacobs, Martin Margiela and A.P.C. It is here that Delicabar opened its doors in November 2003 and that, ever since, its bright terrace and simple interior are normally abuzz with discerning shoppers taking a well-earned break.

The chic eatery was established as an independent venture for talented young pâtissier Sebastien Godard. Former assistant to master pastry chef Pierre Hermé at Fauchon, Godard looks set to garner even more attention here, in his journey away from the conventional French dining formula and into uncharted culinary territory.

The designer responsible for the interior was Claudio Colucci, who divides his time between offices in Paris and Tokyo. Born in Switzerland to an Italian family, Colucci has studied design in Switzerland, London and Paris and includes collaborations with Philippe Starck in his portfolio.

125

Preceding spread: Oversized, high-back sofas make guests feel as though they are children again.
Opposite: Vividly coloured seats look like candy-coated vitamins.

Above: This long, white counter is made of Corian, a durable product by Dupont.

Active in fields as diverse as furniture and environmental design, Colucci approaches interiors in the same way that Godard approaches food: with an air of innovation that made him the ideal man for the job.

As the name suggests, Delicabar offers up an array of mouth-watering delicacies based on fruit, vegetables and chocolate. Nor does the head chef lose sight of the aesthetic appetites of his well-heeled clientele, coming up with dishes that are not only delicious, but also a pleasure to look at. Novel snacks and confections – such as pink salads, fois gras au chocolat, iced teas, apple millefeuille and other tempting pastries – are listed in attractive menus whose contents strike a balance between sweet and savoury. Inside Delicabar, an immaculate white backdrop acts as a foil for a cheerful palette of bright red, pink, purple, green and yellow, bringing to mind both the fresh colours of market-bought produce and the vivid hues of candy-coated vitamins. Dividing the space into separate areas is a shiny white curved bar, the focal point of the interior. 'I created a space with round, soft, melted forms, which are pliant, colourful and pleasant to touch,' says Colucci, who has given these components slightly oversized proportions intended to transport the visitor to a juvenile consumerist world that welcomes, pampers and encourages the shopaholic.

Outside on the terrace, undulating banquettes the colour of new leaves sit under parasols in the winter garden, while light also enters the bar and lounge area through a canopy of glass. 'In France, what people look for most in design is elegance, and then for the history behind the object. It's important that things tell a story, in design and in everything else,' says Colucci, adding that Italians demand instant clarity, as opposed to the French, who aren't bothered if they don't understand everything at first glance. 'You need to give it grace and glimmer,' he explains poetically. 'With this emphasis on history, there's been a tendency towards housing, shops and interiors that are rather conservative.'

126

Architect:	Project:	Location:	Year of completion:
Claudio Colucci Design	Delicabar	Paris, France	2003

Opposite top: The bright terrace at Delicabar is in sharp contrast to the simpler interior of the eatery.
Opposite bottom: Undulating banquettes the colour of new leaves sit under parasols in the winter garden.

This page: Futuristic stools have built-in illumination.

128

Architect:
Claudio Colucci Design

Project:
Delicabar

Location:
Paris, France

Year of completion:
2003

As he points out, minimalism in Japanese architecture and simplicity in Japanese cuisine (which first exerted an influence on French cooking many years ago, giving birth to nouvelle cuisine) have given the younger generations in France a taste for simplicity and originality that currently manifest itself in an emphasis on more contemporary design in shop and restaurant interiors. This recent trend sees the paring away of unnecessary detail in favour of an unadorned style that remains functional yet exudes a particularly French elegance and esprit.

Colucci has the following to say about the concept of Delicabar: 'When people eat delicious food, particularly sweet things, they become more innocent. They fall into a childlike frame of mind. In this interior, I used a long table, big sofas and oversized furniture. Before visitors even realize it, they start to feel smaller, more like children. Eating the food and pastries they really want, they relish a moment of pure bliss.'

INSIDE DELICABAR A CHEERFUL PALETTE OF BRIGHT RED, PINK, PURPLE, GREEN AND YELLOW, BRINGING TO MIND THE FRESHCOLOURS OF MARKET BOUGHT PRODUCE.

Opposite: Claudio Colucci based his palette on the colours of ripe fruit.

Estudio Minim Vilá & Blanch:
El Bosque de Samsung

133

134

Architect: Estudio Minim
Vilá & Blanch

Project: El Bosque
de Samsung

Location:
Barcelona, Spain

Year of completion:
2005

Architect: Estudio Minim Vilá & Blanch
Project: El Bosque de Samsung
Location: Barcelona, Spain

Text by Sarah Martín Pearson
Photography by Stephan Zaurig

Having been commissioned to design the restaurant for Barcelona's 2005 CasaDecor exhibition, Elina Vilá and Agnès Blanch of Estudio Minim drew inspiration from a living forest. CasaDecor, with its focus on interior and furniture design, offers Spanish designers an ideal platform for putting their imaginations to the test, exploring new ideas and coming up with unique presentations. The restaurant project had to please two big-name clients: Samsung Electronics Iberia, a CasaDecor sponsor, and Catalan chef Sergi Arola, holder of two Michelin stars. Vilá & Blanch realized the importance of creating a high-tech atmosphere with a clear reference to Samsung, while also providing a functional space that would allow the chef and his staff, Arola Catering & Hotel Arts, to satisfy all gastronomic expectations. In the words of the designers: 'We had to create a practical space that would also reflect a strong, innovative image of Samsung Electronics. Meanwhile, the restaurant had to fulfil its functional requirements, in order to operate at a high level.'

The space reserved for the project had originally served as the stables of Casa Burés, a modernist house in the Eixample district of Barcelona. When Vilá & Blanch first saw the interior, it was not only completely bare but also damaged by the passage of time. Aiming for a design that would make an impact on visitors, the duo experimented with colour before bathing the entire space in a brisk peppermint-green, a single homogenous hue that left all imperfections visible yet neatly camouflaged by a skin of forest green. Instead of creating a false-walled box to cover up irregularities, they used the existing volumes, surfaces and textures to their own advantage. The next step was to broaden the dining area by demolishing two walls, a decision that precipitated the addition of structural ceiling beams for reinforcement. After installing MDF boards to smooth out the uneven floor, they divided the space into three zones: a bar, a high-tech chill-out area showcasing Samsung products and a main dining room.

135

Vibrant white furnishings in each zone stood out against the green background. Visitors entered the restaurant through the bar, which featured Patricia Urquiola's white Viccarbe stools and a counter clad in white Silestone that curved to form the floor of the chill-out zone before rising to become a table. Backing the bar was Cappellini's white polypropylene bubble-shaped shelving, designed by Ronan and Erwan Bouroullec.

The dining area showed off Vilá & Blanch's key ideas for their experimental approach to the project. Along with the creative use of colour, they employed lighting to shape the ambience they

had in mind. Cool fluorescent tubes distributed at random and at different heights across the ceiling simulated the branches of trees, while small cube lights at floor level added a warm incandescence to the interior. Dimmable lamps allowed the intensity of the lighting to be adjusted as desired.

The dining room, which started off as a wide and rather impersonal space, was divided into more intimate areas by custom-designed screens composed of green-painted wooden poles arranged in a semicircle. Thanks to these movable partitions, the room could be sectioned

Architect: Estudio Minim
Vilá & Blanch

Project: El Bosque
de Samsung

Location:
Barcelona, Spain

Year of completion:
2005

according to use. Cube lamps were positioned at the bases of these screens to enhance their texture, again as a reference to the forest theme. Complementing lightweight chairs in the dining room were custom-designed tables with white Silestone-clad tops. Additional counters in this area were arranged to facilitate service, along with three refrigerators: one for bottles and two larger, American-style Samsung models. In what became almost an independent project, Vilá & Blanch tackled the job of building the open-plan 30-m^2 kitchen.

VILÁ & BLANCH'S ARTIFICIAL INDOOR FOREST WAS A FEAST FOR BOTH EYE AND PALATE.

Opposite: Movable curved screens made of wooden poles painted green divide the interior into intimate areas and emphasize the forest theme.

Above: The bar, where guests are invited to wait before taking their seats in the main dining room, includes a high-tech chill-out zone that showcases Samsung products. A curved screen separates table seating from customers standing at the bar.

The brief asked for a kitchen that would be visible to guests in the main dining area, while also featuring a fireproof wall and a special flame-resistant window for their protection. Fully equipped with electrical appliances by Gaggenau, white Dada furnishings and Silestone working surfaces, the kitchen – in full view of diners waiting for or already enjoying their meals – offered everyone in the room an extra source of entertainment.

Asked to summarize the design, Vilá & Blanch mention four basic points: the creation of an open-plan restaurant, which necessitated the removal of walls; the experimental treatment of colour and lighting; the introduction of mobile vertical elements in the form of screens, for the sake of privacy and a sense of intimacy; and kitchen activities visible from the dining room. All things considered, their artificial indoor forest was a feast for both eye and palate. The scene was one of exquisite meals prepared by Arola Catering arranged on custom-made tables, bustling chefs demonstrating their culinary talents in full view of the diners, and avid enthusiasts of high-tech trying out Samsung's latest electronic devices. A lively happening intended to please one and all.

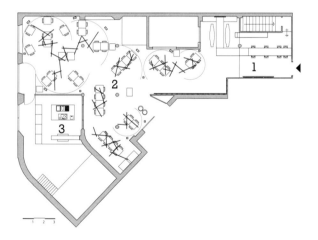

138

Architect: Estudio Minim Vilá & Blanch

Project: El Bosque de Samsung

Location: Barcelona, Spain

Year of completion: 2005

Floor plan
1 Bar
2 Dining area
3 Kitchen

Above: The warm colours of the tiled kitchen are a contrast to the cool green atmosphere of the restaurant. Thanks to a flame-resistant window, diners can watch their meals being prepared.

UNG

BLACK

AND

ANDER

Rockwell Group:
Kittichai

144

Architect:
Rockwell Group

Project:
Kittichai

Location:
New York, USA

Year of completion:
2004

Architect: Rockwell Group
Project: Kittichai
Location: New York, USA

Text by Shonquis Moreno
Photography by Eric Laignel

Outside the hotel, visitors are greeted by a rare species of black bamboo called Phyllostachys nigra. Inside, rows of yellow and violet orchids lit from behind float in tangles within slender jars that adorn a series of white shelves: part abundant pantry, part gorgeous science experiment. Designed by Rockwell Group, Kittichai is a 279-m2 Thai restaurant in New York City's SoHo neighbourhood. The establishment opened in June 2004, replacing an Indochinese-influenced nightspot called Thom, which had previously occupied the ground floor of the 60 Thompson Hotel. Both the new name and the new design – which involved the creation of not only the interior but also waitstaff uniforms and the graphic presentation of food – revolve around the restaurant's world-class executive chef, Thai native Ian Chalermkittichai.

Chalermkittichai's namesake seats 120 in the dining room, 15 in the foyer-like thumbnail of a bar and 40 in outdoor cabanas, weather permitting. Announcing the change of geography at the entrance to the bar, a coarse column rising from the stained wood floor wears the armadillo-like armature of a coconut tree. Between each ring of 'bark', a strip of light shines upwards.

Preceding spread: Lined with shelves containing yellow and violet orchids in slender jars, the bar area is anchored by a column resembling a coconut tree.
Opposite: The focal point of the restaurant is a reflecting pool threaded with invisible cables dotted with orchids.

Left and right: Totems of Thai culture, like the orchid and carved wooden objects, fill niches and line walls.

The flowers held captive in the jars are plum orchids of the genus Phalaenopsis, which are so ubiquitous in Thailand that their colours are depicted on the Thai flag. Rockwell Group architect Diego Gronda added food colouring to the water in which they float in order to give the light pouring through the jars – and filling the room – a warm glow. The space is also dotted with other sorts of treasures of the Thai culture: statuesque heads of Bodhisattvas, carved wood totems and stool-like tables with brass tops (the surface of which is uneven enough that visitors rest drinks there at their own risk).

The design of Kittichai represents the contrast between culture and nature. Smooth white banquettes in the bar are garnished with bolsters clad in black shantung silk, a contrast with the artificial treelike column that doubles as a light source. The bar provides clues to what lies deeper inside the restaurant, while forming a transition from outdoors to indoors and from Kittichai to the sleeker-looking hotel beginning on the floors above.

Beyond the bar, a short, dark corridor leads past the unexpectedly banal lavatories (to which the client assigned no budget) and walls threaded with Thai script in metal cursive letters that tell an excerpted story about the chef's first culinary explorations in his mother's kitchen. On the floor, a carved wood model of a Thai punt is crewed by the flames of white candles. Past the toilet area, a thoroughly traditional and tranquil Thai environment opens up, an intimate dining room fretted with layers of porous wood screens, columns and ceiling beams. Against the wall, cabanas hem the room, backed by red and orange silk fabrics hanging from the walls. Like a chiaroscuro, the interior is echoed by the design of black waitstaff uniforms which are accented with colourful goring. As waiters serve, their garments flutter open to reveal brilliant linings that complement the room.

THE DESIGN OF KITTICHAI REPRESENTS THE CONTRAST BETWEEN CULTURE AND NATURE.

146

Architect:	Project:	Location:	Year of completion:
Rockwell Group	Kittichai	New York, USA	2004

147

Opposite: The head of a Bodhisattva greets those who belly up to the bar.

This page: The dining room is a tranquil Thai interior layered with wooden screens, columns and ceiling beams. Cabanas line the edges of the room. Walls are hung with red and orange silk fabrics.

148

Architect:
Rockwell Group

Project:
Kittichai

Location:
New York, USA

Year of completion:
2004

Details like this make the transformation from the previous space total. The team also worked at a larger scale to evoke a completely different feeling from the former restaurant. The first step was to create a single, unobstructed area at the back of the restaurant by eliminating a wall and running trelliswork beneath the existing ceiling to obscure it. 'Guests don't notice,' says Gronda, ' but half of the main dining room is covered by a tensile structure. Technically speaking, the main dining area is an outdoor space.' Because the existing ceiling looked disjointed and felt oppressive, the Rockwell team used lighting to emphasize the height they did have, including uplighting aimed at silk wall hangings and columns. They also shifted the focus of the room from periphery to centre by inserting a reflecting pool and an 'orchid twirl'.

'This is a feel-good restaurant, full of good energy, and a very spiritual place, ' says Gronda. 'Particular care was taken care with feng shui. A feng shui expert came all the way from Thailand to make sure the restaurant's energies were properly balanced.' To this end, coins have been hidden beneath the wooden floor, a Buddha placed strategically at the entrance, and bamboo selected with special care.

The 'twirl' marks the air above an extremely important element in the interior's composition: a reflecting pool that anchors the centre of the space. The twirl is an unusual display of fresh flowers and light that ascend out of the reflecting pool towards the ceiling.

The twirl, which is the most distinctive element of the design, is an unusual display of fresh flowers and light that ascend out of the reflecting pool towards the ceiling. The orchids are strung as gently as jewels along slender crisscrossing cables, as if waiting expectantly to be buffeted on a breeze. 'Flowers are a big part of Thai culture,' explains Gronda. 'Every single aspect of Thai culture can be related to flowers: a taxi driver will carry flowers in his car, a martini will be brought to you with an orchid, messages left in a hotel bedroom will always be accompanied by a flower.' Diners be warned. You may want to visit a florist before showing up for your reservation at Kittichai.

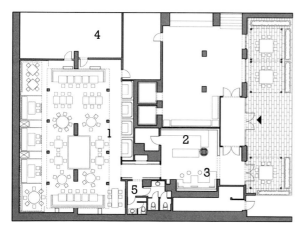

Floor plan
1 Dining area
2 Bar
3 Lounge
4 Kitchen
5 Lavatories

Opposite: Yellow and violet orchids are native to Thailand and mark many mundane transactions in the country.

SHABU-S
A SELECT
OF RAW E
PREPARE
IN JAPAN
BOUILLO

152

154

Architect: Project: Location: Year of completion:
Maurice Mentjens   Thaiphoon   Roermond, Netherlands   2004

Architect: Maurice Mentjens
Project: Thaiphoon
Location: Roermond, Netherlands

Text by Anneke Bokern
Photography by Arjen Schmitz

Visitors to Thaiphoon's website find the restaurant described as a place 'where neon meets religion'. Apart from the decorative statues of Buddha found in the restaurant in Roermond, a town in the southeastern Netherlands, the reference to religion has little to do with reality. Neon, on the other hand, is a different story.

Thaiphoon occupies the ground floor of two residential buildings on a lacklustre street not far from the centre of town. Behind the narrow façade, a long, corridor-like space leads to a resplendent arrangement of Buddha statues at the far end. Furnished in what might be called 'Bangkok Pop', the restaurant displays contemporary lounge furniture cheek by jowl with kitschy elements such as fake crocodile skin and rosy neon lighting.

Responsible for the interior design of Thaiphoon is Limburg-based designer Maurice Mentjens. Working closely with the owner, he developed a spatial concept that included a bar, a restaurant and a private room which could be turn into a club later on the evening. A general lack of interest, however, led the owner to drop that part of the plan. 'In big cities like Amsterdam or Rotterdam, it's very trendy to transform a restaurant into a club later on in the evening,' says Mentjens.

Opposite: Culture clash. White imitation leather with a crocodile-skin motif rubs shoulders with modernist Gimlet bar stools and kitschy chandeliers.

Left: Exterior signals interior. Golden tiles decorate the entrance, and the name of the restaurant appears in a blaze of red neon.
Right: Resplendent on pedestals along the rear wall of the restaurant are several Buddha statues imported from Asia.

'People in Roermond, however, don't seem to like having their chairs whipped from under them so they can dance.' Although Thaiphoon now serves cuisine from all corners of the world, the orginal idea was that of a classic Thai restaurant. 'I've never been to Thailand,' says Mentjens, 'so I pored over some coffee-table books in search of inspiration. What excited me most was the strange mixture of ultramodernism and tradition that seems to characterize life in Asia's big cities.' He took that mixture and developed an interior with a light-hearted Southeast Asian feel to it.

Thaiphoon's entrance, framed in heavy black uprights and brightened by brass-tiled walls, is reminiscent of the gate to an Asian temple. It leads to a bar with a long wood counter and spare, wall-mounted shelving for bottles illuminated by built-in, computer-controlled, neon T-bulbs in red, yellow and blue. Colour – a potential four million shades – bathes the wall in a gradually changing rainbow of pink, blue and violet light quite similar to the bright neon advertising that illuminates the night in Asian cities. The opposite wall, boasting its own blast of Bangkok baroque, is a surface of white imitation leather in a crocodile pattern interrupted by lamps and little fold-down tables for drinks. The sleek line of the bar and an antique Venetian chandelier are all that keep the visitor from imagining himself on the set of a film by Wong Kar-Wai.

Behind the 12-m-long bar is the restaurant, in which crocodile-patterned wallpaper is complemented by simple, red-painted tables and black Tom Vac chairs by Ron Arad. Four openings in a wood-slatted wall running the length of the room lend access to stairs descending to the toilets, the cloakroom and the private room. Painted entirely black, the private room has a high, shiny, Barrisol stretch ceiling. Hanging from the ceiling at the centre of the space is a contrasting cluster of red Plexiglas lamps by Kartell, which seem to float like jellyfish above the table and are reflected in the ceiling.

Architect:	Project:	Location:	Year of completion:
Maurice Mentjens	Thaiphoon	Roermond, Netherlands	2004

157

Opposite top: Mentjens created with Lagotronics the
lighting concept for the bar wall, where bottles are bathed
in up to 4 million colour variations.
Opposite bottom: In the bar, the imitation leather
is one of the references to Asia. A 12-m-long counter
of oak is resolutely minimalist.

This page: Red lamps by Kartell lend the private room
a suitably sultry atmosphere. A semi-see-through slatted
screen divides this room from the restaurant area.

The combination of black and red in the small room is evocative of Japanese lacquer-work boxes and of the famous 'red lantern'. To heighten the sensuous atmosphere of the private room even more, occupants need only shut off all access to the space by closing the sliding doors. Beneath a 5-m-high glass roof at the back of the restaurant is the conservatory, a no-smoking area that offers a fine view of the garden outside. The rear wall of the conservatory was painted by Utrecht artist Gonnette Smits, whose professional name is Muurbloem (Dutch for 'Wall Flower'). The painting is in various shades of violet with floral highlights in gold and black. The golden Buddha statues in front of it resemble baroque angels adorning a Christian altarpiece.

Like the menu with its international dishes, the interior of Thaiphoon is a true Eurasian mix. Rather than making a futile attempt to copy authentic Asian design, Mentjens has consciously played with Asian clichés, but not those that refer to the classic minimalism sometimes associated with oriental design. His take on Thailand zeroes in on the trashy pop aesthetic of Southeast Asia's mega-cities, which are the current image radiated by urban Asia. In this sense, the interior design of Thaiphoon is as Dutch as French fries in peanut sauce or as Asian as 'Chinese' chop suey, a recipe invented in America.

'WHAT EXCITED ME MOST WAS THE STRANGE MIXTURE OF ULTRAMODERNISM AND TRADITION THAT SEEMS TO CHARACTERIZE LIFE IN ASIA'S BIG CITIES.'

Maurice Mentjens

Architect:	Project:	Location:	Year of completion:
Maurice Mentjens	Thaiphoon	Roermond, Netherlands	2004

159

Opposite: Elegant black rest rooms are furnished
with Alape washbasins.
This page: Mentjens designed the folding tables. Charcoal-
coloured ceramic tiles enhance the cool atmosphere.

164

Architect:
Francesc Rifé

Project:
NuBa

Location:
Barcelona, Spain

Year of completion:
2004

Architect: Francesc Rifé
Project: NuBa
Location: Barcelona, Spain

Text by Sarah Martín Pearson
Photography by Eugeni Pons

Situated in a former warehouse in the university district of Manresa, Spain, NuBa caters to a highly varied clientele and thus includes not only a tapas bar, but also a more traditional restaurant. Francesc Rifé approached the design of the 300-m² space in his usual rational manner. An atmosphere of elegance pervades an interior of blacks, greys and whites, in which an orderly composition of superimposed planes highlights a diversity of textures. The interior design revolves around a series of barred elements used mainly to organize the space. These take the form of either wood or metal grilles that communicate in the designer's distinctive visual language.

Rifé's initial concern was a warehouse confined within blind walls that were allowing no daylight to penetrate the interior. The solution was a series of windows and a framework of metal grilles with randomly arranged parallel bars, which introduce a dynamic into the otherwise static façade. 'We started with the idea of opening the location towards the exterior, and then added the framework to achieve a heightened air of privacy and a sense of movement,' says Rifé. Smoked-glass window panes soften the flow of natural light that bathes the interior.

Preceding spread: In the main dining room, barred partitions organize the space and improve the acoustics.
Opposite: Lining the periphery of the dining room are custom-designed tables with steel bases painted grey and metal tops clad in black leather. Dining chairs were designed by Francesc Rifé for Viccarbe.

Left: Windows facing the street feature metal grilles with randomly arranged parallel bars. Smoked-glass panes filter excess sunlight and increase the diner's sense of privacy.
Right: Rifé opened the restaurant to passers-by with a series of windows and a framework of metal grilles. Concealed among the windows are the main entrance and, between bars, the logo, which appears to be lit from behind.

Concealed among the windows are the main entrance and, between bars, the logo, which appears to be lit from behind.

The visitor crosses a glass-panelled hall to a centrally positioned, dark-granite welcome desk, which divides the restaurant into two areas: tapas bar and dining room. Like a runway that begins at the main entrance, the granite desktop unfurls to meet the floor, visually separating bar from restaurant and contrasting with the grey shade of the epoxy-resin flooring used throughout the space. The desktop also extends to form the counter of the tapas bar; cutting across the room lengthways, the bar offers a bright display of snacks, as well as a glimpse of the kitchen. Backing the bar, a surface of black steel sheet and smoked glass continues the neutral palette, while the front of the bar displays wood panelling bearing grey-painted stripes of different widths. Purpose-designed luminaires in the form of long black cylinders hang above the counter. Bar stools and chairs with seats in black-painted oak are Francesc Rifé's designs for Viccarbe.

Custom-designed tables lining the periphery of the dining room have steel bases painted pale grey and metal tops clad in black leather. At the far end of the room, access to the toilets is enhanced by a plate-glass window with the same type of framework used for the façade, complete with door and logo, this time in vinyl lettering. Rest-room doors concealed in a cream-coloured wall panelled in the same material as the front of the bar blend with the resin floor.

Catching the eye in the main dining room are the barred partitions that divide the space into zones while also improving the acoustics of the room. Not only do these grey grilles act as screens between tables, creating more intimate corners; they also isolate two private dining rooms at the back, which can be closed off with additional sliding doors. One area of the dining room is furnished with custom-built tables that line a long bench parallel to the windows and partially upholstered in black fabric. Other tables are tucked between grilles, cosily private but still open to a partial view of the surrounding space.

166

Architect:	Project:	Location:	Year of completion:
Francesc Rifé	NuBa	Barcelona, Spain	2004

167

Opposite: The restaurant is divided into two areas: a tapas bar, with informal seating at the counter; and a dining room furnished with comfortable chairs and tables. The plate-glass door at the far end lends access to the toilets. The interior also includes a small Zen garden.

This page: A dark-granite counter extends like a runway from the reception desk at the main entrance to become the top of the tapas bar. Cylindrical black-metal pendants illuminate the counter.

168

Architect: Project: Location: Year of completion:
Francesc Rifé   NuBa   Barcelona, Spain   2004

Attention to detail is obvious in every aspect of NuBa's interior design. Rifé took care to gear the aesthetics of the materials he selected to the monochromatic scheme, while also custom-designing all furnishings and taking a special interest in the lighting project. He says that 'the industrial-design work we have developed concludes the project, giving the space its ultimate touch, without acquiring a leading role'. Especially noteworthy are the designer's purpose-made dining tables; his cylindrical metal lighting fixtures, which illuminate the bar; and the main light source, a continuous ceiling-mounted structure that hangs above the tables lining the exterior wall and unifies the two principal sectors of the restaurant. Additional lighting has been cleverly integrated into small rectangular slits in the ceiling.

Satisfied with the results, Francesc Rifé says that 'aspects such as soberness, together with balanced and well-proportioned volumes, dominate the space as a whole. Ultimately, these are the same ideas I try to portray in all my projects.' Featured in this elegant restaurant design are a balance of geometric volumes, a pleasantly uniform level of lighting, functional spaces, and harmonious combinations of materials. Together with the stripy graphic leitmotif and the serenity of soft greys interspersed with black and white, these components contribute to a relaxing dining experience – whether it be an informal tapas snack at the bar or a more elaborate meal in an intimate nook of the dining room.

'ASPECTS SUCH AS SOBERNESS, TOGETHER WITH BALANCED AND WELL-PROPORTIONED VOLUMES, DOMINATE THE SPACE AS A WHOLE.'

Francesc Rifé

Opposite: Metal grilles allow tables to be tucked away for more privacy, while still offering a partial view of the surroundings. Grilles are also used to isolate two private dining rooms that can be closed off completely with additional sliding doors.

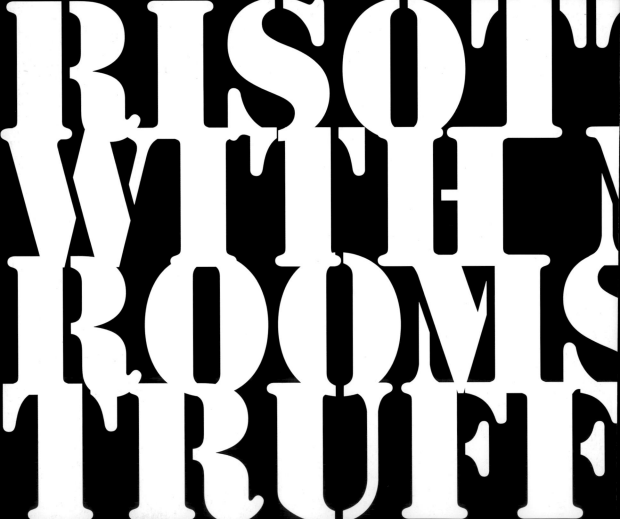

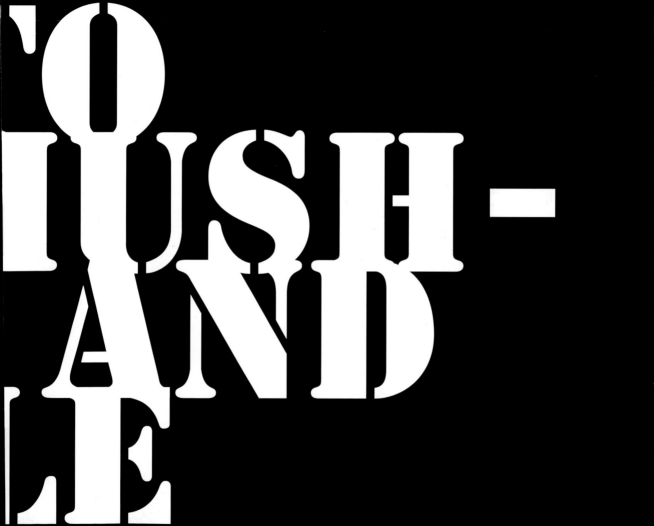

Puresang:
Ciné Città

174

Architect: Project: Location: Year of completion:
Puresang   Ciné Città   Genk, Belgium   2005

Architect: Puresang
Project: Ciné Città
Location: Genk, Belgium

Text by Anneke Bokern
Photography by Kristien Wintmolders

When a geologist found large coal reserves near the Belgian town of Genk at the beginning of the 20th century, the rural area enjoyed a boom. The Winterslag mines were opened, and within a few decades the population of Genk had increased tenfold. Many new inhabitants were foreign miners and their families, including quite a few Italians.

The boom has long since passed. Coal mining is no longer profitable, and the mines were shut down in 1988. For decades, this 180-hectare site lay unused, until an investor recognized the potential of the gloomy industrial remains. Today, the site accommodates a multiplex cinema with ten theatres, a couple of cafés and the Ciné Città restaurant.

What better name for a restaurant housed in a motion-picture complex than Ciné Città? But we can also read on the website that the name 'refers to the many Italian immigrant miners'. The place where pitmen once removed coal dust at the end of a shift now serves up vitello tonnata and osso buco, for the restaurant occupies the washrooms of the former mine.

175

Opposite: A basic palette of muted colours is enhanced by a walnut floor, walnut wall panelling, black furniture and red highlights.

Left: Furniture found in the restaurant reappears in the brasserie, although here in the colours of the Italian flag. Walls are covered with large black-and-white photos of Italian film stars.
Right: A staircase leads from the restaurant level to the mezzanine. Hanging at the lower level is a huge still from the film Goodfellas, which is framed by striking strip lights.

Designer Will Erens of Puresang was ambivalent about the surviving remains: 'One hurdle, for example, was the presence of a few old tiles found on the wash room walls, which had to be preserved. So there's a white-tiled base to the wall in the brasserie.' These tiles, however, are the only element that harks back to the history of the mines. Elsewhere, the Antwerp design studio has created a warm interior in which the raw aesthetic of the industrial building converges with an abundance of wood and retro-kitsch lamps in muted shades of green with red highlights. Ciné Città consists of two sections: the brasserie, for pre- or post-cinema drinks and snacks; and the restaurant proper, with a newly built mezzanine floor that caters to groups. The mezzanine not only enlarges the capacity of the restaurant, but also offers a magnificent view of the old pits – a scene that, according to Erens, extends into the distance with the air of a film set.

The twin themes of film and Italy run through the whole restaurant. In the brasserie, white bistro tables stamped with the name Ciné Città are combined with classic wooden chairs painted in the colours of the Italian tricolour – in culinary terms, a palette of mozzarella, tomatoes and olives. The room is lit by dramatic crystal chandeliers, which continue the red note of the scheme, along with eight impressive '70s lamps above the bar. The bar, painted army green to complement the rough brickwork of the stripped walls, is lower and deeper than its more conventional cousins, allowing customers to eat at the counter. A collage of cabinets displaying bottles covers the back wall.

Black-and-white photos of Italian film stars from the '50 and '60s, the heyday of the Cinecittà studios in Rome, line the brasserie walls, forming a stylistically confident leitmotif that also embellishes the adjacent restaurant. One illuminated wall displays a large still from the film Goodfellas. 'That's a private joke between the owner and myself,' says Erens. 'As children we were neighbours. The boys on that photo take us right back to our youth.'

Architect:	Project:	Location:	Year of completion:
Puresang	Ciné Città	Genk, Belgium	2005

177

Opposite: Through the slatted oak screen masking the mezzanine floor, diners have a wonderful view of old mining areas that can also be seen by those entering the restaurant through the front door.

This page: In the brasserie, red chandeliers rub shoulders with spherical lamps from the '70s. The extra-low bar is suitable for eating dinner.

178

Architect:
Puresang

Project:
Ciné Citta

Location:
Genk, Belgium

Year of completion:
2005

In contrast to the floating floor of the brasserie, the restaurant has an oak floor, which matches one panelled wall. 'Chic yet cosy' is the intended effect, and the original roughness of the industrial buildings has almost completely vanished. Lighting is furnished by alternating black and white crystal chandeliers supplemented by pink lights that glow behind the panelled wall. Simple black chairs with leather seats in red, brown and white are arranged around black tables.

The mezzanine is separated from the restaurant by a slatted oak screen that acts as an optical division without obstructing the diner's view. Mezzanine walls feature black MDF panelling below a mirrored strip that encircles the space. Above this reflective band are some 200 framed photos of Italian actors interspersed with scenes from spaghetti westerns. Here, as elsewhere in the interior of Ciné Città, lamps – star-shaped chrome pendants from the '50s – serve as a focal point, while paying nostalgic tribute to mid-20th-century Italian films.

In this interior Puresang has acknowledged past and present, while creating a thoroughly cogent synthesis of three keynotes: Italian films, contemporary lounge design and the industrial aesthetic. The most original and distinctive reference to the coalfields however, is not visible to guests. Because the utility shaft was not large enough to contain the central-heating ducts, Puresang drilled a hole straight through to an old mineshaft, where a constant temperature of 17 degrees Celsius supplies Ciné Città with a fine source of fresh air.

THE PLACE WHERE PITMEN ONCE REMOVED COAL DUST AT THE END OF A SHIFT NOW SERVES UP VITELLO TONNATA AND OSSO BUCO, FOR THE RESTAURANT OCCUPIES THE WASHROOMS OF THE FORMER MINE.

Opposite: Different sizes of olive-green cabinets provide shelving in the bar. The designers scraped away old plaster to reveal the original red-brick walls.

MUSHI
AND
SPINAC
LASAG
WITH
CIABAT

ROOM

H

N

E

ARLIC

TA

183

184

Architect:
SHH Associates

Project:
The Hub

Location:
London, England

Year of completion:
2005

Architect: SHH
Associates
Project: The Hub
Location: London, England

Text by Edwin van Onna
Photography by Morley von Sternberg

Pupils forced to join long queues or even to leave the premises to eat lunch poses a potential problem for any school. Matters worsen when kids purposely avoid a school cafeteria they call 'tatty, rough and downbeat', a description once overheard at the Acland Burghley Secondary School in north London. It was obviously time for a more dynamic place and one geared to a teenager's idea of a cool canteen. SHH Associates – experienced in bar and restaurant design – took such ideas seriously and launched a plan with diverse colour- and graphic-coded zones for different types of eating. Pupils can hang out at a trendy snack corner, grab a salad from a bar furnished with poufs, or have lunch while surfing the Net in the IT zone. Outside on the terrace, a hideaway with the look of an underground train carriage encourages face-to-face encounters. Built in the 1960s, the existing cafeteria was an unattractive space with a layout that did not allow some 450 pupils an hour to queue and eat lunch in a relaxing atmosphere. Older pupils often made off for neighbourhood establishments, a practice that led to poor eating habits, littering and mischief.

Preceding spread: On a wood platform outside the school building, metal 'pods' offer pupils a cosy, sheltered place to have lunch.
Opposite: 'Floating' benches and tangerine walls invite kids to enjoy a face-to-face moment.

Left: A sliding partition facilitates the transition from the snack corner to an outdoor patio with bar tables and soft poufs.
Right: All poufs in The Hub were designed by Inside Out. Not only more durable than chairs with backrests, they also encourage a lively air of social exchange.

Together with a group of pupils from age 14 to 16, SHH explored new lunch-related options. 'Only by having the children directly involved did we fully understand what the space needed to cater for,' says architect Neil Hogan. 'The whole process was quite an eye-opening experience for any designer, especially in terms of the emphasis the children put on the sociable aspects of the space and the wish to interact at all times.' He explains that the idea was part of the Joinedupdesignforschools initiative, run by The Sorrell Foundation, an organization that studies 'how good design can improve school life by listening to the voices of the pupils themselves'.

SHH's multifunctional, rationally organized plan takes various users into consideration: kids looking for a quick snack before going out to play, older children who like to linger over lunch and chat, pupils with a preference for hanging out in groups, and so forth. 'Certain areas needed to process quick dining needs at speed, others had to be comfortable and relaxing, and some spaces are deliberately quiet and restful,' says Hogan.

Obstacles liable to slow circulation were eliminated. 'Pupils enter The Hub down a main stair,' says the architect, 'with the canteen's doors already opened, sealed back seamlessly

Architect:	Project:	Location:	Year of completion:
SHH Associates	The Hub	London, England	2005

on magnetic closers to become part of the corresponding wall graphic.' Facilities such as servery units, wastepaper baskets and radiators have been integrated into wall panels. And colour-coding improves circulation while also identifying each zone. The snack corner is yellow, the diner zone red, the bar green, and the internet area orange: bright colours chosen by the pupils, who also had a hand in the interior design of each space. Wall graphics range from skateboarding or frolicking teens to tube trains and radio waves – active images directly linked to the lifestyle of those attending Acland Burghley.

The use of upholstered stools and poufs throughout the various zones represents another decision taken with the wishes of the focus group in mind. 'In terms of usage, they offer more flexibility for kids to choose their own layout,' says Hogan, adding that poufs without backrests allow youngsters to face in various directions. Soft seating was in the pupils' brief. And poufs are more durable than chairs, which are subjected to the stresses of tipping, tilting and so forth. He also points out that poufs 'offer advantages in the sense that they sit completely under the tables and keep the human scale very low, giving the appearance of less clutter in the room'.

Opposite top: For financial reasons, wall graphics were silk-screened in black on coloured laminated panels.

Above: Facilities such as wastepaper baskets, vending machines and storage units have been fitted flush into the wall of the snack corner. Lamps above bar tables are Ethel pendants designed by One Foot Taller.

A noteworthy aspect of the architectural concept is the use of outdoor space. A sliding partition separates the snack corner from the outside zone, which includes a patio with standing-height tables and poufs. Interior flooring of yellow linoleum merges nicely with the yellow concrete surface outdoors, where a gleaming object reminiscent of a tube train offers protection from inclement weather. 'We were looking for a stylish way to encourage all-weather use of the outdoor space,' says Hogan. The shelter, which consists of freestanding metal segments, is open at both ends. Stainless-steel benches extend from interior walls that flash a bright tangerine welcome. 'The pods are very inclusive, in the sense that they allow groups of friends to hang out together in a confined space,' says Hogan, 'giving them a real sense of ownership of that space.' Supporting the segments is a wood platform, which features a cutout for the trunk of a full-grown willow tree that provides this area with a private spot and, in the summer, functions as a cooling canopy. Sitting beneath the willow is like hiding in the folds of grandma's apron.

'THE WHOLE PROCESS WAS QUITE AN EYE-OPENINGEXPERIENCE FOR ANY DESIGNER.'

Neil Hogan

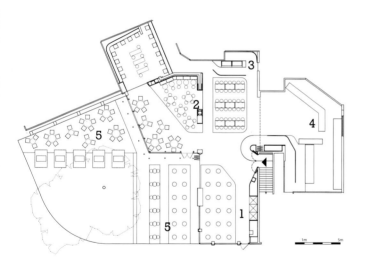

Architect:	Project:	Location:	Year of completion:
SHH Associates	The Hub	London, England	2005

189

Floor plan
1 Snack Zone
2 Diner Zone
3 Bar
4 Counter
5 Break out Space

View from the indoor dining area showing the wood platform and the metal pods. In the foreground are bucket-seat Bellini chairs by Heller.

Jason Jenkins & The Finevibe:
Kantinery

194

Architect:
Jason Jenkins &
The Finevibe

Project:
Kantinery

Location:
Düsseldorf, Germany

Year of completion:
2005

Architect: Jason Jenkins & The Finevibe
Project: Kantinery
Location: Düsseldorf, Germany

Text by Edwin van Onna
Photography by Jason Jenkins

During the day a cosy lunchroom for the business crowd and at night a hip space for gatherings of up to 200 people. At Kantinery, domesticity and efficiency have a tight, symbiotic relationship. German firm Jason Jenkins & The Finevibe developed a comprehensive concept for this informal restaurant in the port area of Düsseldorf, where a nutritious lunch is underlined by fast, friendly service.

Jason Jenkins & The Finevibe has taken a concept similar to that of an archetypal canteen and translated it into a contemporary, multifaceted restaurant. Kantinery exhales a casual sigh that envelops estate agents and media bosses who – with drinks they've fetched from an erstwhile supermarket display case – sit on floral poufs or at lace-decorated tables. After developing the name, concept, logo, menu and interior of Kantinery, designer Jason Jenkins 'styled the staff'.

The restaurant occupies a former flour mill on Plange Mühle. Inside, rough brick walls and walled-up windows refer to the building's industrial past, a time when technicians moved between cube-capitalled columns, maintaining the grinding machines and other equipment.

Preceding spread: In Düsseldorf, diners soak up the industrial atmosphere of a former flour mill. A band of coloured displays made from zinc and Plexiglas makes a harmonious entity of the original brick walls.
Opposite: The interior design features a striking contrast between the virginal white of the dining room and the domestic 'patterned' ambience of the lounge area.

Left: Guests feel right at home seated at plain picnic-style tables that are decked out with well-used trays, edges curling, and plastic doilies.
Right: By illuminating the concrete columns, Finevibe added the illusion of extra height to the room.

In its present conversion, as Kantinery, the building – although not at the centre of the local media zone – welcomes a clientele that comes mainly from Düsseldorf's Media Hafen.
The 315-m² space melds a central dining area of virginal white with a lounging area that recalls the snug comfort of grandmother's lap. The former, which borders the entrance, features orderly rows of white laminated tables and benches that seat 140 guests. Illumination comes from pendants with large white shades. Demarcating this area is a smoothly finished concrete floor and shotcrete-clad walls. A large self-service unit – a remodelled supermarket acquisition – invites diners to fetch their drinks.

The encircling lounge area has a parquet floor and 'warmer' furnishings: brown tweed sofas, floral-patterned rugs and cosier seating areas with patterned poufs and plastic-bucket-seat chairs. 'I was really excited when I found these beautiful rugs,' says Jenkins. 'They are between 30 and 40 years old and look like huge, handmade, Bavarian-style tapestries.' He recalls pictures and cushions of 'the kind that grannies once made' and compares the pixelated patterns to 'a bad computer screen'. Although decades old, the rugs have not faded. Indeed, they have been washed in tea to get the desired vintage look.

The interior seems to turn its back on high-end design in favour of second-hand finds mixed with purchases from IKEA. Why? 'It was partly budget,' says Jenkins, 'but mainly the wish to have a warm, welcoming, homely interior – and, in this case, designer furniture just didn't do that for me.' Jenkins clearly sees the future of restaurant design as an extension of his recipe for Kantinery. He predicts a move 'away from overloaded form and design' and dining rooms in which people can 'enjoy the secret of the finevibe that is created between people'. Happiness should be a product of togetherness, Jenkins believes, rather than the result of well-designed surroundings.

In line with his philosophy, he has not rigidly executed the contrast between pragmatism and cosiness. It's more a matter of a funky mix of styles than of an irreconcilable conflict.

Architect:	Project:	Location:	Year of completion:
Jason Jenkins & The Finevibe	Kantinery	Düsseldorf, Germany	2005

Opposite top: It's easy to locate toilets that beckon with all the charm of a red-light district.

Opposite bottom: Furniture includes second-hand, but[ton]... chairs and round IKEA tables with [specia]lized bases.

This page: Thanks to two types of flooring, concrete and [p]arquet, the transition betw[een] dining and lounge areas [i]s clearly visible.

Architect:
Jason Jenkins & Finevibe

Project:
Kantinery

Location:
Düsseldorf, Germany

Year of comp
2005

On Kantinery's picnic-style tables, trays with their edges curling form a background for plastic doilies that, says an enthusiastic Jenkins, 'emphasize the domestic aspect and are so practical. Plastic fantastic! The material is reusable and easy to clean. I found it in a hardware store. It comes on a big roll, and I cut it to fit the trays. I also used it to cover tables on Kantinery's outdoor terrace.' Striped fabric on the majority of the cubic poufs is geared to the professional nature of lunchtime guests.

Playing a decisive role at Kantinery are wall-mounted light boxes. Jenkins initial idea was to install, between windows, an uninterrupted row of light boxes along the entire perimeter of the room. He wanted to enliven the space 'through the dynamics of the stripe and the white light'. After looking at the briefing again, Jenkins realised that in the evening the venue would be used to host dinners and events quite unrelated to the style of the daytime Kantinery. He implemented the lighting plan in the form of coloured displays that can be used to showcase, for example, the Kantinery logo or the name of a firm that rents the space temporarily.

Light has also been used, indirectly, to indicate the location of the toilets. A red glow flowing into the restaurant from the entrances to the toilets designates their presence without signage. The message is clear and every bit as enticing as the suggestive gleam of colour that beckons visitors to the city's red-light district.

'THE FEEL OF THE INTERIOR SHOULD BE WARM, WELCOMING AND HOMELY– AND, IN THIS CASE, DESIGNER FURNITURE JUST DIDN'T DO THAT FOR ME.'

Jason Jenkins

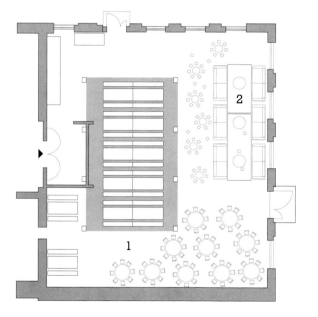

199

Floor plan
1 Dining area
2 Lounge

Opposite: In addition to the floor, concrete has been used to finish ceilings, columns and damaged walls.

RAS
ASFOI
LENTI
SOUP

George Henry Chidiac Architects: Café Blanc

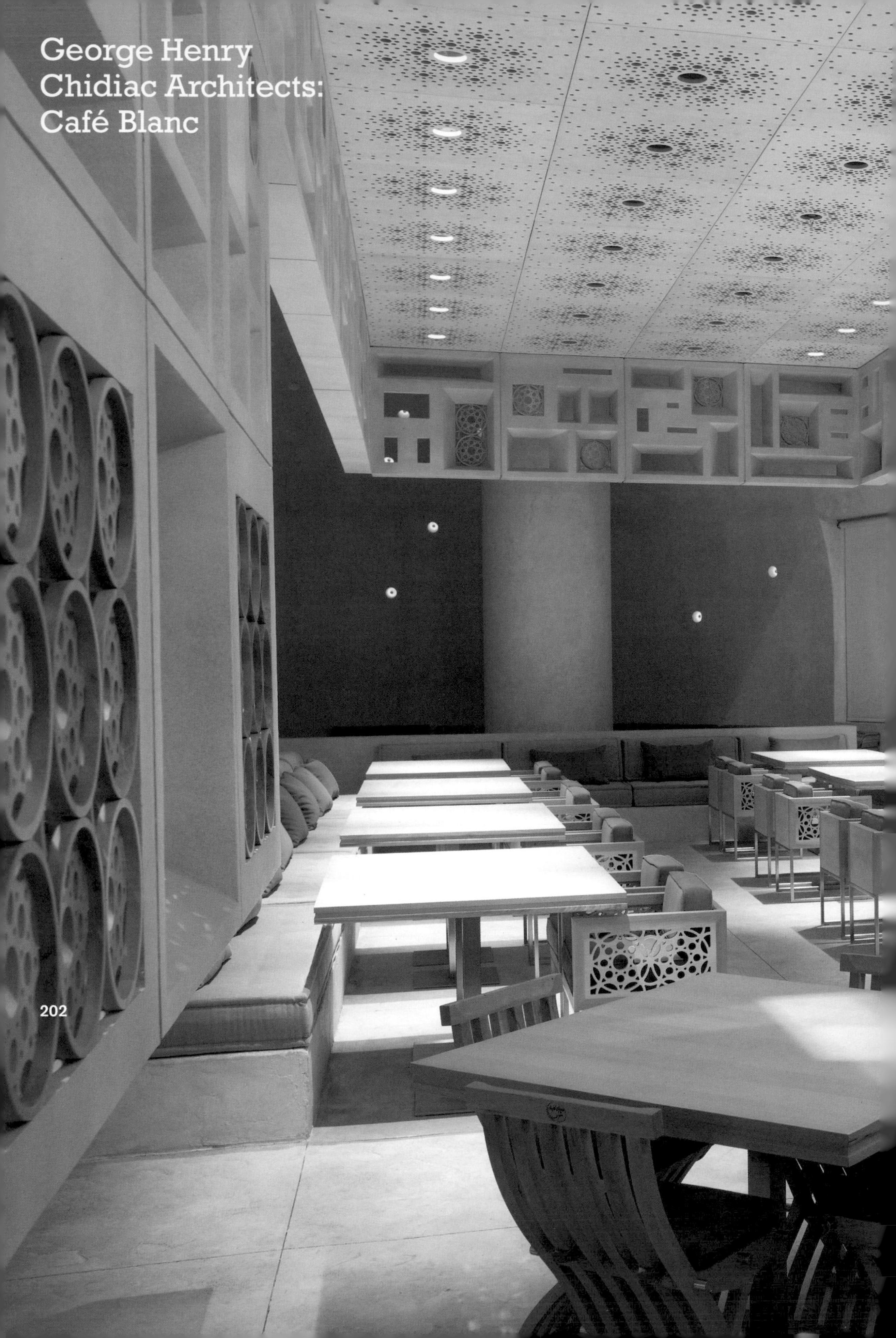

204

Architect: George Henry
Chidiac Architects

Project:
Café Blanc

Location:
Beirut, Lebanon

Year of completion:
2005

Architect: George Henry
Chidiac Architects
Project: Café Blanc
Location: Beirut, Lebanon

Text by Shonquis Moreno
Photography by Imad el Khoury

Lebanese restaurant Café Blanc in Beirut is a modern filigree scattered with illuminated niches, carved walls embroidered with light, and vaulted ceilings crowned with the pinpricks of remote stars. Actually, Café Blanc is less white than it is filled with the palest colours of the earth and a vivid Mediterranean turquoise – hues that seem to announce the bright end of a seaside day. Starting underfoot with his tinted concrete floor, his box of clean geometries and a reverent use of pattern, George Chidiac of George Henry Chidiac Architects has designed a contemporary architecture to house a traditional cuisine. 'The environment had to be young, cool and inspiring, but it had to appeal to both the young and the old,' says Chidiac. 'This was achieved by combining traditional materials and effects with modern techniques.'

Although Café Blanc is a casual eatery – where visitors can order a cup of café blanc, a piece of Turkish-delight cheesecake or even a narghile (a graceful, water-filled oriental pipe, also called a hookah, that is used for smoking tobacco flavoured with rose, apple or honey, for instance), while playing backgammon with friends – it is also a formally sophisticated space, despite a concomitant minimalism.

205

Preceding spread and opposite:
Café Blanc's design is porous, inspired by old Lebanese dwellings.

Left and right: Chidiac used 1-x-1-m modules in four patterns across the walls of the restaurant. Modules are made from tinted, computer-cut, plaster-coated MDF and sheathed with a solid timber called moucharabieh or adorned with carved ornaments.

The forms of the 670-m2 interior (250 m2 of which is occupied by the kitchen) were based on those found in old Lebanese dwellings, says Chidiac. They hark back to a time when entire families used to live, eat and sleep in a single room as a matter of course. The constant need to economize on space led inhabitants to carve small openings in the thick walls of the house and to use the resulting niches for storage. These walls were originally made of mud and rubble, which prompted the architects to craft 1-x-1-m modules in four patterns that they used to give the restaurant texture, porosity and an elegant partitioning system. When rotated, the modules – made from computer-cut, tinted-plaster-coated MDF – can be positioned in 16 configurations for a highly varied range of compositions across the walls of the restaurant. 'Over the modules we placed a solid timber called moucharabieh,' explains Chidiac, 'or added a carved ornament, so that when sunlight filters into the premises an embroidered pattern is reflected onto the tables and chairs, giving the space a romantic, oriental atmosphere.' The moucharabieh pattern is rooted in the orange-tree blossom from which the white Lebanese coffee called café blanc is distilled; its arabesque of circles creates a floral motif that is repeated throughout the interior.

Overhead, the ceiling looks like a continuous surface made of lace. It consists of 1-x-1-m perforated panels made from laser-cut, maple-veneered MDF, which hides all air-condition-ing ducts and grills, as well as light fixtures, fire sprinklers and smoke detectors. Below, flourishes of carved wood are contained in generously boxy benches and armchairs.

Architect: George Henry
Chidiac Architects

Project:
Café Blanc

Location:
Beirut, Lebanon

Year of completion:
2005

207

Opposite top: Even the lavatories have a romantic, oriental atmosphere.
Opposite bottom: The lounge is modelled after a Turkish bath.

Above: Perforated 1-x-1-m ceiling panels are made from laser-cut, maple-veneered MDF.

208

Architect: George Henry
Chidiac Architects

Project:
Café Blanc

Location:
Beirut, Lebanon

Year of completion:
2005

The lighting scheme was designed by PS Lab Projects, but Chidiac is responsible for the fixtures, which resemble filters, laces and textiles. These fixtures, the furniture and other accessories within the space were all custom-made for the restaurant by the architects.

A lounge area inspired by the Turkish hamamet, or bath, forms a smooth, curved, high void between the dining room and the lavatories and provides space for visitors to smoke or drink cocktails. Beyond the lounge, a single central room contains the lavatories, each of which has one cylindrical loo on either side of the room. These perforated stalls are shaped like narghiles, with their pierced ceilings. Again, light passes through the ceiling the way it would pass through lace curtains or the water-worn passages of an underwater grotto lit only by reflected light. Alongside the restaurant is a boutique that sells china, narghiles, spices, soaps and costumes: the designs of famous Lebanese artists who have come up with modern renditions of traditional objects. It is packaging that echoes the interior architecture – taking what is best of the old and making it new.

GEORGE CHIDIAC AIMED FOR A 'YOUNG, COOL AND INSPIRING ENVIRONMENT' THAT WOULD APPEAL TO GUESTS OF ALL AGES.

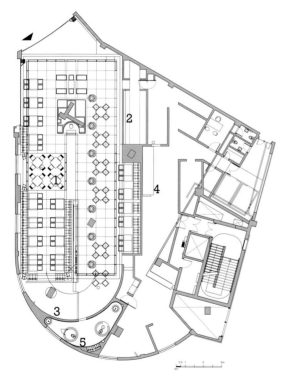

Floor plan
1 Dining area
2 Bar
3 Lounge
4 Kitchen
5 Lavatories

Opposite: The perforated stalls of the toilets, also laser-cut, are shaped like narghiles; as a result of the pierced effect, escaping light embroiders nearby walls.

SE
OOD

212

214

Designers:
Steve Leung Designers
and Alan Chan Design
Company

Project:
MX

Location:
Hong Kong, China

Year of completion:
2005

Designers: Steve Leung Designers and Alan Chan Design Company
Project: MX
Location: Hong Kong, China

Text by Masaaki Takahashi
Photography by Ulso Tsang

One of the true homes of Chinese cuisine is Guangdong Province, at whose edge lies the animated city of Hong Kong, its geographical location immaterial to its role as the heart of the region. Food is its lifeblood and has a culture all its own; locals will tell you that life in this metropolis is simply impossible to imagine without the odd hour spent sipping fragrant tea and chatting over a plate of steaming dim sum. Clustered along streets throughout the city, dim sum restaurants present only one problem: there are so many that you'd be forgiven for not knowing which one to try first.

For the novice, a good place to start might be a series of latest renovated Quick Service Restaurants opened by Maxim's Group, a company famous for managing one of the largest fast-food chains on the island. According interior design an importance ignored by many of its competitors, Maxim's recent addition to its ranks looks to uphold the tradition of adopting exciting new design in a quest to give the customer a completely new dining experience. Given the Chinese name of MX means 'the beauty of the heart', therefore, it's undoubtedly the overall décor is 'hearty-driven' and filled up with different kinds of heart-shape graphics.

215

Preceding spread: The white interior at MX,
in which Steve Leung and Alan Chan skilfully incorporated
Asian art, has the look of a gallery.

Opposite: Leung collaborated with brand consultant
Alan Chan to create the interior.
Left: Passionate red exploding-hearts logo gives
the glazed façade a retro-chic look.
Right: The same logo embellishes the cash desk.

The first restaurant of this chain, called simply MX, can be found tucked away in Hong Kong's North Point district, an area largely unknown to sightseers.

Low prices in this part of town – where vendors at open-air markets sell fish, flowers and apparel – reflect the location of North Point: at the end of a tramline on a ferry route seldom used by tourists. Hong Kong-born interior designer Steve Leung gave MX its distinctive look, and the logo of the restaurant was the work of famous brand consultant Alan Chan, also a native of the city. Chan has worked on graphics in the international arena, both in Asia-Pacific, and his café and other productions in Japan have proved extremely popular among Tokyoites. Leung's office, on the other hand, is gaining in popularity all over China and now employs over a hundred staff, including a large number of qualified and experienced architects and interior designers who work in major cities throughout the country.

Nearly keeping pace with the architectural side of the business is interior design, as evidenced by an increasing involvement in residential, retail and restaurant projects.

Alan Chan, being the Brand Consultant and Creative Director of this rebranding program, he partnered with Steve Leung and his company for the overall interior, making minimalism the key to the interior, Leung skilfully incorporated Asian art and culture into the design, creating an environment that reflects the fusion of traditional Chinese cuisine and contemporary fast-food fare. The atmosphere at MX is more reminiscent of a sophisticated café than a casual snack bar. To capture the essence of Chinese culture while giving it a contemporary twist, they paired the bright white tones of purity and innocence with the passionate red of MX's exploding-hearts logo for a retro-chic look. They also emphasized the different zones in the restaurant through selective use of the two colours, contrasting the white dining area with a red cash desk and food-service section.

Designers:
Steve Leung Designers
and Alan Chan Design
Company

Project:
MX

Location:
Hong Kong, China

Year of completion:
2005

217

Opposite top: The trendy fibreglass chairs and tables at MX are custom-made.
Opposite bottom: A relaxing atmosphere is what Hong Kong's contemporary crowd is looking for in a café.

This page: Leung and Chan have catered to the Hong Kong penchant for eating while watching TV, a habit that has taken hold in many parts of our high-tech world.

A colour with strong roots in Chinese tradition, red symbolizes good health and fortune. At MX, it has been employed in the plastic shades of large table lamps and on the ceiling, where red covers exposed ductwork and forms an exciting foil for the off-white of dropped-ceiling areas, walls, chairs and counters. Elsewhere, numerous smaller versions of the lamps work to give the place a cosier feel. The red logo softly evident in the lampshades also extends boldly across the glazed façade in a vivid burst of hearts that reaches out to passers-by. Brand identity is maintained through subtle use of hearts throughout the space.

Along one wall and several columns, custom-made mosaics further enhance the positive atmosphere generated by the warm overtones of the logo. Trendy fibreglass furniture, simple yet ergonomically designed, enhances the casual atmosphere. On surfaces above banquettes and booths is work by 16 Asian artists, whose 'heartfelt' contributions add interest to the décor and heighten the desired mood. Relaxation is an important theme, coupled with an accent on delivering food with straightforwardness and sincerity – from the heart. Sitting at a counter seat, the first-time guest suddenly notices tiny TV screens set into the countertop, a feature that

Designers:	Project:	Location:	Year of completion:
Steve Leung Designers and Alan Chan Design Company	**MX**	**Hong Kong, China**	**2005**

expresses the Hong Kong penchant for dining in front of the box and that is part of Leung's and Chan's strategy to make diners feel more at home. Telly and food, even in a restaurant: what could better illustrate the changing culture of dining in today's high-tech world?

The message conveyed by MX is that – while the flavour of Chinese food itself may not change very much in the foreseeable future – it's likely that we will be seeing more restaurants showcasing this type of fresh, new design: a space that embodies the East-meets-West style so suited to the cultural melting pot that is Hong Kong.

BOTH LEUNG AND CHAN HAVE SKILFULLY INCORPORATED ASIAN ART AND CULTURE INTO THE DESIGN.

219

Opposite: A heart-shaped feature made from mosaic tiles continues the theme.
Above: Work by 16 local artists is displayed in the restaurant.

KHYBER
LEGENDA
KHYBER
LAMB MA
OVERNIG
EXOTICS
AND ROA
IN A CLAY

Khosla Associates
and tsk Design:
Khyber

224

Designers:
Khosla Associates and
tsk Design

Project:
Khyber

Location:
Mumbai, India

Year of completion:
2006

Designers: Khosla Associates
and tsk design
Project: Khyber
Location: Mumbai, India

Text by Shonquis Moreno
Photography by Pallon Daruwala

Although the interior design for Mumbai restaurant Khyber is based on an undeniably dramatic geographical divide, the collaborative process behind it blurs the lines between graphic and interior design. Created by architect Sandeep Khosla of Khosla Associates and his wife, graphic designer Tania Singh Khosla of tsk Design, Khyber, which means 'across the river' or 'divide' in Aramaic, is named for the Khyber Pass, a 53-km incision through the frozen Hindu Kush mountain range that both connects and divides the East (India and Pakistan) and the West (Afghanistan, Iran and Turkey). As mincingly narrow as only three metres and lined with precipitous shears, this violent terrain has served as a strategic portal for both mercantile and martial invasions, starting in 326 B.C. with an incursion by Alexander the Great and continuing with visits from Persian, Mongol, Tartar and British armies, to name a few.

Located in the Bandra neighbourhood of North Mumbai, the Khyber restaurant is the daughter outpost of an eatery that has been serving rich Mughlai or 'frontier' cuisine – Khyber Rann and Kheema Se– for over 40 years, food born at a crossroads of nomads, merchants and warriors on the move.

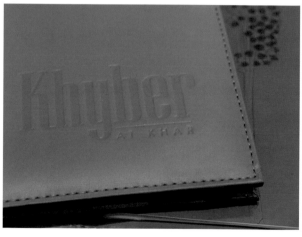

225

Preceding spread and opposite: The interior design of Khyber, a restaurant in Mumbai, is based on the notion of a geographical divide, the Khyber Pass, and is the product of a collaboration between graphic design and architecture.

Left and right:
Signage and menu detail.

The original, traditionally decorated space featured paintings by famed Indian artists, including M. F. Husain and Anjolie Ela Menon; the new Khyber draws on the region's rich traditions (particularly textile), weaving them together in a contemporary way aimed at a younger clientele dominated by tourists and professionals from the area's creative, advertising and media industries.

Emphasizing the dual character of the Pass, as both partition and connector, the interior is dominated by a dramatic central axis in the form of a reflective copper 'ribbon' that is laser cut with a pattern derived from a tribal Afghani kilim and lit from within. 'We were keen on interpreting Khyber as a divide or passage that would form a strong central axis slicing through the space horizontally and vertically. A central walkway dividing the seating areas of restaurant symmetrically, a dramatic decorative ceiling feature hovering over it, and the culmination in central staircase linking the two floors emphasizes the importance of this axis', says Sandeep. This ribbon runs along the ceiling, dividing the space visually, providing symmetry for the room (below it, seating is arranged on either side) and determining the path of a walkway through the space. It also helps to conceal air-conditioning ducts, thus maximizing the low ceiling height. The pattern cut into the copper comes from a 16th-century Anatolian tribal rug. 'In Islamic art and in Indian and Afghani cultures, the Tree of Life is symbolic of the passage between earth and heaven, between life and the ideal world,' says Tania. 'The Khyber Pass is a physical passage, whereas the Tree of Life is a symbolic one. Since the Khyber Pass has historically been associated with war and bloodshed, we were looking for a positive interpretation of it, one about life and peace.' The designers altered the pattern considerably by modifying its proportions and scale and accommodating it to the laser technology used to cut the copper.

This translation of traditional images continues on two walls bearing paintings that were digitally printed onto antiqued porcelain tiles to evoke frescoes. One is an interpretation of A Female Acrobat (1815), a Persian oil painting that hangs in the Victoria and Albert Museum. The second, entitled Fath Ali Shah, is by Mizra Baba (1798).

226

Designers:
Khosla Associates and
tsk Design

Project:
Khyber

Location:
Mumbai, India

Year of completion:
2006

227

Opposite: Running along the ceiling is a copper ribbon that has been laser-cut with a Tree of Life pattern from a 16th-century Afghani kilim; the pattern, which originally symbolized an intangible transition, here represents the Khyber Pass.

This page: Representing prosperity in the midst of chaos is the 18th-century Persian portrait that has been digitally reproduced on one wall.

228

Designers:
Khosla Associates and
tsk Design

Project:
Khyber

Location:
Mumbai, India

Year of completion:
2006

'We chose these works for the incredible and bewildering detail and ornamentation of the rendering,' says Tania. 'This style of 18th- to 19th-century Persian painting represents a period of glamour, luxury and prosperity in the otherwise tumultuous history of Iran. The intricacy and lavishness of the paintings embraces influences from Persia to Kashmir and spans the various geographical influences that occur in the cuisine at Khyber.'

Despite floor-to-ceiling glazing on three sides of the interior, windows provide unexceptional views. The team took this opportunity to warm the space with silk curtains lit from beneath. Colours – earthy dark browns, olive greens and dusty blues contrasted with burnt orange – and textures (both rough and refined) in the space were suggested by the climate, terrain and tribal art of the region. Embodying the roughness of the terrain, a porcelain tile resembling crude black slate was used. This hygienic, stain- and wear-resistant material suggests and replaces one that is porous and difficult to maintain.

Khyber's upper floors are threaded together by a dramatically modern central staircase with a steel frame and treads of 40-mm Burma teak. 'Railings are in the edge polished frameless toughen glass to give the stair a light feeling,' says Sandeep, ' while preventing dust from the feet of customers and staff from falling onto the service stations below.' Thanks to its central location, the staircase frames and highlights the ceiling motif. Taken together, ceiling, stair, graphics and finishes consolidate Khyber's multiple geographical and cultural origins and connect its past with what is still to come. The view forward, if not out the windows, is a rather exquisite one, reminding diners that the thing that divides must necessarily connect.

'THE INTRICACY AND LAVISHNESS OF THE PAINTINGS EMBRACES INFLUENCES FROM PERSIA TO KASHMIR AND SPANS THE VARIOUS GEOGRAPHICAL INFLUENCES THAT OCCUR IN THE CUISINE AT KHYBER.'

Tania Singh Khosla

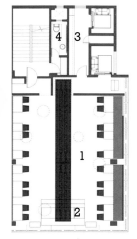

Third floor

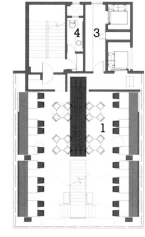

Forth floor

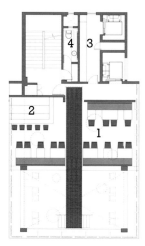

Fifth floor

229

Floor plan
1 Dining area
2 Bar
3 Pantry
4 Lavatories

Opposite: Huge windows that offer poor views are softened with bright curtains which adhere to the earthy palette of the interior. Leading to the upper floors is a grand, steel-framed, glass-and-teak staircase.

RaiserLopesDesigners:
Olio e pane

234

Architect:
RaiserLopesDesigners

Project:
Olio e Pane

Location:
Metzingen, Germany

Year of completion:
2005

Architect: RaiserLopesDesigners
Project: Olio e Pane
Location: Metzingen, Germany

Text by Anneke Bokern
Photography by Frank Kleinbach

The southern German town of Metzingen, population 20,000, is unflatteringly referred to as 'the capital of skinflints', because it is home to some 50 outlet stores run by top-end brands like Boss, Joop, Strenesse, Escada, Bally and Reebok, which attract German bargain hunters, as well as shoppers from Switzerland and France. 'It's a strange place,' says Hartmut Raiser of RaiserLopesDesigners. 'A small river, the Erms, cuts right through the middle of Metzingen. The old town lies on its right bank, and on the left you have the outlets.'

Also on the right bank, at a sort of interface between the two worlds, a glass pavilion stands on a square next to the river. It houses a restaurant, Olio e Pane, whose realization was the collaborative project of two firms: Riehle and Partners Architects and RaiserLopesDesigners. 'We were involved in the planning of the building from very early on,' says Raiser. 'We contributed to the ground plan and changed some things in the original design.'

The result is a simple, two-tiered pavilion that floats above Lindenplatz on its rectangular base. The pavilion seats an equal number of customers inside and outside, where a spacious terrace embraces three sides of the building.

235

Opposite: RaiserLopesDesigners designed the small tables. Chairs are by Arper.

Left: All graphics, including the name of the restaurant, are by are by RaiserLopesDesigners. Brilliant red-neon lettering is seen above the edge of the pavilion roof.
Right: When viewed from the outside, the building – designed by Riehle + Partner of Reutlingen – looks like a simple glass case with a spacious terrace.

The name of the restaurant is displayed in large red lettering on the glass façade, and in summer this façade opens up fully, allowing interior and terrace to merge. Kitchens situated at one end of the glass cube are visible through a large window in the side wall. Adjoining this area is a bar with a large high table and accompanying stools that seat up to 14 customers. The bar lends access to the restaurant area, which accommodates about 70 diners.

Construction of the restaurant was financed by Holy, a firm belonging to the Hugo Boss Group, which runs a large proportion of the outlets across the river. 'The firm wanted to give something back to the town,' explains Raiser. 'For a long time now, they've been trying to pull outlet shoppers into the old town as well.' He says that prior to the arrival of Olio e Pane, what Metzingen had to offer were plain, traditional restaurants with oak furniture and the like. A discriminating public, including many foreigners with an eye for designer apparel, were looking for something a bit trendier. 'But at the same time, of course, we didn't want to deter local inhabitants. We wanted a restaurant where outlet shoppers and locals would mix and mingle.'

With those thoughts in mind, they opted for a classic, somewhat subdued design with lots of wood and few strong colours. The idea was to create a 'cave within the glass case'. Contrasting with the brightness of glass is dark-brown, pressured-treated beech, which has been used on floor, ceiling, staircases and outdoor decking. To dim the interior even more, black, floor-length curtains can be pulled over the large glazed surfaces of the pavilion. The curtains, a product of Swedish manufacturer Ludvig Svensson, are made from a coarse fabric that diners can see through during the day, although passers-by do not have a view of the interior. 'In Swabia, this is important, for people have a Calvinist work ethic and prefer not to be seen sitting around in a restaurant in broad daylight,' explains Raiser, somewhat tongue in cheek. The wall over the bar has been given a coat of blackboard paint, as have the walls next to a window into the kitchen, providing surfaces for displaying the menu of the day.

Architect:
RaiserLopesDesigners

Project:
Olio e Pane

Location:
Metzingen, Germany

Year of completion:
2005

Opposite top: The name of the restaurant is written
on the side of the building in large red letters.
Opposite bottom: The view through the glass façade allows
passers-by to see the interior and even read the menu, which
is written on a slate-coloured surface above the bar.

Above: The interior features a palette of dark colours
and white tablecloths. The only thing that stands out
is the illuminated red bar.

The only contrast to the dark browns, greys and blacks of the interior are found in the bar, where illuminated shelves with recesses for bottles have been painted red and the bar front is a glazed wall of gleaming scarlet. This wall is not just decorative; it also functions in the manner of a traffic light. As Raiser points out, it lies on the same axis as the front door. 'Guests entering the restaurant come straight towards it, and they are meant to wait until being shown to their tables.'

RaiserLopes designed the small dining tables, each of which – when combined with black chairs by Arper – seats two people. Thanks to their size, these pieces are easy to arrange in various configurations. 'You see that a lot in Italian bistros,' says Raiser. Other subtle references to Olio e Pane's Italian cuisine are tiny olive branches, moulded into tabletops made of MDF, and the olive-leaf pattern that RaiserLopes applied to the outer walls of the kitchen. No further allusions to Italy are made, for neither architects nor client wanted an interior that would be too kitschy for Boss employees or the smart shopping set. Olio e Pane perfectly complements the classic understatement of designer brands.

238

Architect:	Project:	Location:	Year of completion:
RaiserLopesDesigners	Olio e Pane	Metzingen, Germany	2005

'WE WANTED A RESTAURANT
WHERE OUTLET SHOPPERS
AND LOCALS WOULD MIX
AND MINGLE.'

Hartmut Raiser

Opposite top: An eye-catching element is the low bar,
made of red glass and lit from within.
Above: The minimalist design continues in the toilet area,
where tubes of light inserted into the walls are covered
with elongated tiles.

242

243

244

Architect: Abelardo
Gonzalez Arkitektbyrå

Project:
World Hockey Bar

Location:
Stockholm, Sweden

Year of completion:
2004

Architect: Abelardo Gonzalez Arkitektbyrå
Project: World Hockey Bar
Location: Stockholm, Sweden

Text by Edwin van Onna
Photography by Åke E:son Lindman

'Face-off' has got to be the official greeting of the World Hockey Bar in Stockholm. Devoted exclusively to ice hockey, this restaurant designed by architect Abelardo Gonzalez evokes images of a real stadium. Visitors eat in an 'arena' or follow the culinary action from comfortable bucket seats high in the 'stands'. Large TV screens display videos of major hockey matches or VJ performances.

The architect links surfaces finished in raw concrete and steel to the theme of the restaurant, calling 'the roughness of ice hockey is used as a metaphor in the choice of materials and textures'. Dominating the World Hockey Bar is a sporty aesthetic whose bold red accents get the adrenalin pumping – even more so since the Swedish hockey team grabbed gold at the Winter Olympics in Turin.

The brief stressed a virtual concept that could be applied to a number of locations. 'We proposed a spatial prototype unique in its design. If successful, it was to be used in different cities – in Russia, Europe, the USA, and Canada – well known for their hockey teams,' says Gonzalez. 'The initial site was to be a former cinema in Stockholm, built in 1950.'

Preceding spread: Furniture in the restaurant is geared to the theme of ice hockey: Philippe Starck's Cam El Eon chair resembles a shoulder pad, and tabletops have puck-shaped rubber inlays.

Opposite: Lines formed by recessed neon lighting indicate the layout of the rink.
Left and right: Seated in the sunken hockey rink, guests can watch legendary games displayed on various monitors.

The concrete skeleton of the elongated, partially underground volume is still recognizable. 'The original concrete structure featured columns, such as those we found inside some walls,' explains Gonzalez. 'We exposed the raw concrete to heighten the contrast between well-finished detail and unfinished surfaces.' Mentioning the granite layers uncovered in the 'excavation' of the site, he points out that 'it's possible to see the granite remains in the way down to the toilets'.

The new plan revolves around restaurant and bar areas distributed over several levels. Centrally situated is a sunken area – the hockey rink – which accommodates 200 guests and is enclosed by transparent Plexiglas 'boards' and large advertisements. A central aisle leads directly to a staircase in the stands that ascends to the bar.

According to Gonzalez, the concept is based on the layout of an authentic hockey rink. 'The space consists of different zones, inspired by the pattern of zones at a hockey rink. Each has its own function: the bar, a space for the sale of merchandise, the combined restaurant and bar, and so on.' Interestingly, as you move farther into the restaurant the atmosphere becomes calmer, zone by zone. You find the oval bar in the entrance area overflowing with regulars, a far less boisterous air in the restaurant, a real sense of relaxation in the stands and, by the time you reach the bar, an unexpectedly cosy ambience.

The ice-hockey theme has been carried through to the smallest detail. Gonzalez drew inspiration from Stockholm's Globen Arena, as well as from a Swedish team, the Malmö Redhawks. Certain flooring, for example, resembles that of a locker room, while other floors display logo stickers or colourful neon lines indicating the layout of the rink. References to the sport appear in the seats of red chairs and bar stools that resemble hockey gloves, in tabletops with rubber inlays and in puck-shaped trays. Furniture in the arena and upper-level bar includes chairs, designed by Philippe Starck for Driade, that look very much like players' shoulder pads.

Architect: Abelardo Gonzalez Arkitektbyrå

Project: World Hockey Bar

Location: Stockholm, Sweden

Year of completion: 2004

247

Opposite top: The glazed treads of the staircase in the stands offer a view of the toilets, which are located deeper in the building.

This page: The subterranean atmosphere of the World Hockey Bar is reinforced by walls and ceilings finished in a dark-grey insulating material behind steel grids. Framing the entrance to the cloakroom is an enormous visor of the type used on ice-hockey helmets.

Architect: Abelardo
Gonzalez Arkitektbyrå

Project:
World Hockey Bar

Location:
Stockholm, Sweden

Year of completion:
2004

And framing the entrance to the cloakroom is an enormous visor of the type used on ice-hockey helmets.

Daylight enters the space only from the main entrance. Artificial light, including that emitted from spots built into the floor, determines the mood, although large illuminated TV screens also serve as virtual windows to the world outside.

The subterranean atmosphere is reinforced by walls and ceilings finished in a dark-grey insulating material behind steel grids that are also used to partition off the stands. These grids – which support TV screens, monitors, spots and the movable VJ cubicle that towers 5 m above the floor of the restaurant – form a leitmotif for the whole interior. 'The steel structure gives an expressionistic effect, one that invites people to come in and that accentuates the dynamic impression of what's going on,' says Gonzalez. 'With its conceptual accent, it communicates a sense of freedom as to how the space can be divided up.'

Nowhere does the space convey a feeling of enclosure. The glazed treads of the staircase in the stands even offer guests a view of the catacombs, where – even deeper in the building – one finds not only kitchen and toilets, but also a games room with comfy chairs and sofas. From the rest-room area you can see the restaurant, and vice versa. Thanks to this visual link, the staircase fulfils a dual function.

A special detail is urinals that feature glass panes in front of monitors displaying videos. Here the player whose well-aimed spurt hits the glass and eliminates his opponent, symbolically that is, is not sent to the penalty box.

'THE ROUGHNESS OF ICE HOCKEY IS USED AS A METAPHOR IN THE CHOICE OF MATERIALS AND TEXTURES.'

Abelardo Gonzalez

249

Floor plan
1 Dining area
2 Bar
3 Cloak room
4 Storage

Opposite: Even deep in the catacombs beneath the stands, visitors can view hockey games on various monitors.

253

EXIT

254

Architect:
Marcel Wanders Studio

Project:

Location:
New York, USA

Year:

Architect: Marcel Wanders Studio
Project: Thor
Location: New York, USA

Text by Anneke Bokern
Photography by Inga Powilleit
Photo styling by Tatjana Quax

Customers who visit the Thor restaurant in
New York in the hope of finding the Norse god
Thor and his hammer are in for a disappoint-
ment. Unrelated to Norse mythology, Thor is quite
simply an acronym for The Hotel on Rivington.
The restaurant is part of this 21-storey, glass-clad
building on Manhattan's Lower East Side. Both
hotel and restaurant opened in 2004.

The interior of the restaurant, with its private
lounge, was created by Dutch designer
Marcel Wanders. Asked about the demands
of the project, Wanders says, 'Overall, I was given
a free hand.' His main focus was the location of the
hotel. The glass tower stands in the middle of a
run-down, working-class district that is evolving
into a mecca of nightlife. The hotel is boxed
in by old tenement buildings.

'It is a very particular part of the city,' says
Wanders. 'A few years ago, hardly anyone came
here. We wanted to draw New Yorkers'
attention to it.'

Wanders' plan was to contrast the seedy charm
of the Lower East Side with the feel of chic luxury.
'Amidst all the rubble and the ruins in the area,
I wanted a high-quality design. This was no place
for minimalism.

Preceding spread and opposite: Visitors entering Thor walk over
a red carpet and through a white, cave-like structure that takes
its shape from Wanders' Egg Vase, which he designed in 1997.

Left: Black bar stools designed for Thor currently belong to
Cappellini's New Antiques collection. The turned legs and curved
shapes of these and other pieces of furniture at Thor lend
a vintage air to the restaurant.
Right: A skylight 7 m above the dining area draws daylight into
the restaurant, while also offering a view of the surrounding
neighbourhood, studded with fire escapes.

All the surfaces had to be special.' Wanders covered the restaurant façade in tiles of differing shades of grey, which merge discreetly with the aesthetic of the area. The entrance itself, however, illustrates what he means by 'special': visitors enter Thor through a cave-like white pavilion with a red floor and arching walls. On closer scrutiny, the construct reveals itself as an enlarged horizontal version of the small Egg Vase that Wanders designed in 1997. 'That's right. Inspired by a condom filled with hard-boiled eggs, the vase was the model for the restaurant. I think its form is very beautiful.'

Once inside, you are immediately struck by the wallpaper, which covers the walls and ceiling of the entire restaurant. A special design from the Wanders Wonders collection, it features hexagonal elements in a complex pattern of geometric and floral forms. Enhancing a stark palette of black and white are minor accents of yellow, red and gold. Wanders explains his Hexagon wallpaper as a personal interpretation of microcosms and macrocosms. 'You find the smallest of details resembling the largest of structures. This is life according to its underlying DNA.'

The colours of the wallpaper pervade the entire interior of the restaurant, which is bathed predominantly in shades of cool white, grey and black. Tucked into the lounge area, behind a large window overlooking the street, are low, dark-brown Bottoni sofas and chairs, pieces designed by Wanders and produced by his furniture company, Moooi. They offset the expressive wall covering. The bar, which also balances minimalism and ornament, has a front covered in laminated tiles – again with a floral pattern in grey and white – and simple, unobtrusive glass shelves for displaying bottles.

256

Architect:	Project:	Location:	Year of completion:
Marcel Wanders Studio	Thor	New York, USA	2004

257

Opposite top: In the rest rooms, the flirtation with kitsch continues. The porcelain figurine is a traditional product of Delft pottery manufacturer De Porceleyne Fles, here in a new context created by Marcel Wanders.
Opposite bottom: Delft Blue with a twist: The sink, also produced by De Porceleyne Fles, is a new design by Marcel Wanders. Traditional tile motifs overlap one another to form a seemingly random pattern.

This page: Virtually everything that appears in the interior of Thor was designed by Marcel Wanders. The only other designer involved was Maarten Baas, whose Smoke series is represented in objects such as the black chandelier with a missing arm.

Architect:
Marcel Wanders Studio

Project:
Thor

Location:
New York, USA

Year of completion:
2004

Like the wallpaper, bar stools, chairs and restaurant tables flirt with old-fashioned daintiness. Black wooden furniture has turned legs, horizontal bars and lightly curved shapes. Although Wanders initially had these pieces made especially for Thor, they are currently a part of Cappellini's New Antiques collection. In the restaurant, the chairs are combined with light-grey banquettes, which line the perimeter of the room. The 7-m-high walls in this space are topped by a huge overhead window, and it is the view beyond this window that catches the eye, for it looks out on the backs of the surrounding tenements, with their crisscross of fire escapes. 'From the restaurant, you see New York's backside,' says Wanders 'It's very impressive.' Adding to the contrasts, Wanders has placed a black steel 'outhouse' (the American term for an outdoor lavatory) in the middle of the restaurant. The slightly crooked construction conceals the staircase to the basement toilets, the only place furnished with objects not designed by Wanders: two black armchairs and a chandelier from the Smoke series by Maarten Baas. A very elaborate picture in a lavish gold frame hanging in this space includes a collage of countless Wanders' objects and a portrait photo of the designer in profile. If this is over-the-top ornament, it has my vote.

> **'AMIDST ALL THE RUBBLE AND THE RUINS IN THE AREA, I WANTED A HIGH-QUALITY DESIGN. THIS WAS NO PLACE FOR MINIMALISM. ALL THE SURFACES HAD TO BE SPECIAL.'**
> Marcel Wanders

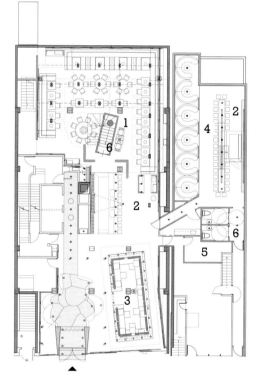

Floorplan
1 Dining area
2 Bar
3 Lounge
4 Private room
5 Cloak room
6 Lavatories

Opposite top: A warped 'outhouse' of black steel takes centre stage in the dining area and lends access to toilets in the basement.
Opposite bottom: The front of the bar is clad with purpose-designed laminated tiles. Along with Wanders' Hexagon wallpaper, which fills the walls and ceiling of the restaurant, these tiles exemplify the Dutchman's anything-but-minimalist interior.

McDonald's
Most served dish:

MCCAFÉ SPECIALI ARE CAK SWELTS, COFFEE, CAPPUCC SHAKES FRAPPES

TIES

ES,

NO,

ND'

262

263

264

Architect:
Costa Group

Project:
McDonald's

Location:
Milan, Italy

Year of completion:
2005

Architect: Costa Group
Project: McDonald's
Location: Milan, Italy

Text by Sarah Martín Pearson
Photography by Moreno Carbone

Famous since the '90s as one of Italy's pioneer drive-in McDonald's, the Cinisello Balsamo Street restaurant in Milan has recently been remodelled by Costa Group according to plans that are intended for implementation all over the country in due time. The Milan establishment is housed in a building with an aluminium-clad façade and wide windows. The ground floor occupies an area of 400 m², while the upper level, which is dedicated exclusively to children, has a 150 m² indoor area and an outdoor terrace.

McDonald's, a leader in the international food-services sector, asked the architects not only to renew the look of its Italian outlets, but also to make them more comfortable by incorporating a general sense of wellbeing, cosiness and relaxation. Says Luigi Benvenuti of Costa Group: 'We tried to create a place like a living room, more homely and cosy, leaving behind the stereotyped concept of the McDonald's we all know.' The project, seen as a prototype for Italy alone, included the introduction of a new 'concept area', the McCafé, which represents a break from the traditional fast-food scheme. Separated from the main dining area, the innovative McCafé – part coffee bar, part lounge – has a casual ambience underlined by comfy upholstered seating.

Opposite: At McDonald's in Milan, faux-leather armchairs in mauve are a feature of the internet corner, where surfers are greeted by a 'pixelated' wall seemingly stacked with firewood and fronted by a twisting sculpture that resembles a gnarled piece of driftwood.

Left: Backed by a minimalist arrangement of dark wooden slats, a stainless-steel logo lit from behind offers a slickly renewed image of the brand.
Right: All graphics, also this graphic on the wall, are the work of Maurizio Benassi.

'The new McCafé was introduced as a separate area to create the sensation of walking into one's favourite living room,' says Benvenuti. 'Custom-designed elements, such as artisanal ceiling lamps and a counter made by a renowned sculptor, add personality to the McCafé.' Costa Group's purpose-designed chairs feature chromed bases and faux-leather upholstery in mauve. The counter, made from an aluminium alloy, is the work of Pietro Ravecca, and Mara Mastrosanti crafted the lamps above the bar.

Colour was an essential aspect of the overall concept. Warm, relaxing shades of brown, purple and beige have been combined with vibrant accents of orange and yellow. Benvenuti says that his team wanted to welcome customers into a 'real place', an adult-orientated space that corresponded to their daily lives. 'We wanted to create a public dining room where people would find both a casual atmosphere and a chic ambience.' It was to be a restaurant ideal for a quick lunch, but also a place to go during leisure hours, just 'to chill-out in a relaxing environment'.

A study of the original layout led them to divide the main dining area into zones that range from informal, communal seating arrangements to more intimate spots. Tables positioned diagonally in the middle of the room, close to the main counter, are separated from the rest of the dining area by light walls that act as screens, partitioning the interior so that all is not revealed at first glance. The aim was 'to give clients a new sensation' by eliminating what used to feel like an impersonal fast-food venue and replacing it with 'a clearly recognizable space'. Among the light walls are bar-seating areas for quick snacks. Tables arranged around the perimeter of the room are illuminated by rectangular, pleated ceiling lamps which add a touch of cosy elegance. The dining room continues to unfold around the staircase area. Still in line with the concept of home are a large family-size table and benches in untreated wood, a more private area with upholstered seating next to the wall, and a large chandelier over the staircase.

266

Architect:
Costa Group

Project:
McDonald's

Location:
Milan, Italy

Year of completion:
2005

267

Opposite top: Downstairs, a family-size table of untreated wood is lined with benches on both sides. This area of the restaurant also offers customers smaller tables with padded seating and teardrop pendants for illumination.
Opposite bottom: A new concept is the McCafé, where the clientele – ensconced in a comfortable, casual atmosphere – can relax and savour coffee and pastries in style.

Above: Not just another McDonald's fast-food clone, the Cinisello Balsamo Street outlet boasts illuminated partitions that heighten intimacy; comfortable padded seating; and pendant lamps and toasty colours for an extra touch of warmth and cosiness.

Architect:
Costa Group

Project:
McDonald's

Location:
Milan, Italy

Year of completion:
2005

'THE MOST IMPORTANT MESSAGE WE WANTED TO PASS ON WAS TO TAKE LIFE EASY IN A QUIET AND COSY PLACE – AS A WAY TO COUNTERACT THE OUTSIDE FRENZY.'

Maurizio Benassi

Graphics, which are the work of Maurizio Benassi, convey the corporate image and company values of McDonald's. 'Illustrations, graphic elements and photographs interact with customers to recall the idea of taking a break and recovering lost moments,' says Benassi. His designs are based on music: Louis Armstrong's What a Wonderful World and New Kid in Town by the Eagles. Scrawled on the walls, the lyrics of these songs, along with related images, suggest serenity and relaxation. Applied to the wall of the staircase are a large illustration of playful children, a smattering of seemingly unconnected words and an overlapping slogan in pastel orange and yellow. Benassi added the names of big cities to the illuminated partitions in the dining room for a dash of international flavour, while further promoting the theme of relaxation by posting messages on the walls such as 'Are you hungry?' and 'Take it easy'. He explains that the idea of 'taking life easy in a quiet, cosy place' coloured the entire project. It was a way 'to counteract the outside frenzy'.

The results of the refurbishment are impressive: a new image for McDonald's in Italy, a space that is surely more appealing to the majority of customers, and a concept that demonstrates an admirable emphasis on wellbeing. Many people who may have never considered entering a fast-food establishment – thinking bad food, bad design, bad atmosphere – may now be tempted to experience a newly conceived space that looks unexpectedly inviting, to spend a few minutes relaxing with the kids and a couple of Happy Meals, and, undoubtedly, to wander into the McCafé for a coffee.

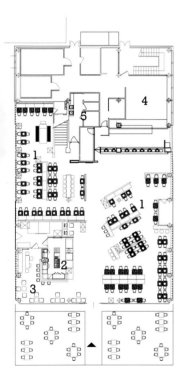

269

Floor plan
1 Dining area
2 Bar
3 Lounge
4 Kitchen
5 Lavatories

Opposite: Although the restaurant functions according to the tried-and-true McDonald's formula, this establishment is marked by an added degree of privacy and comfort, thanks to the warm atmosphere and the division of the space into several distinctively designed and illuminated dining areas.

DAN DAN
NOODL
WITH
A BLAC
SESAM
FILLIN

Hashimoto Yukio Design Studio: Kamonka Ueno Bamboo Garden

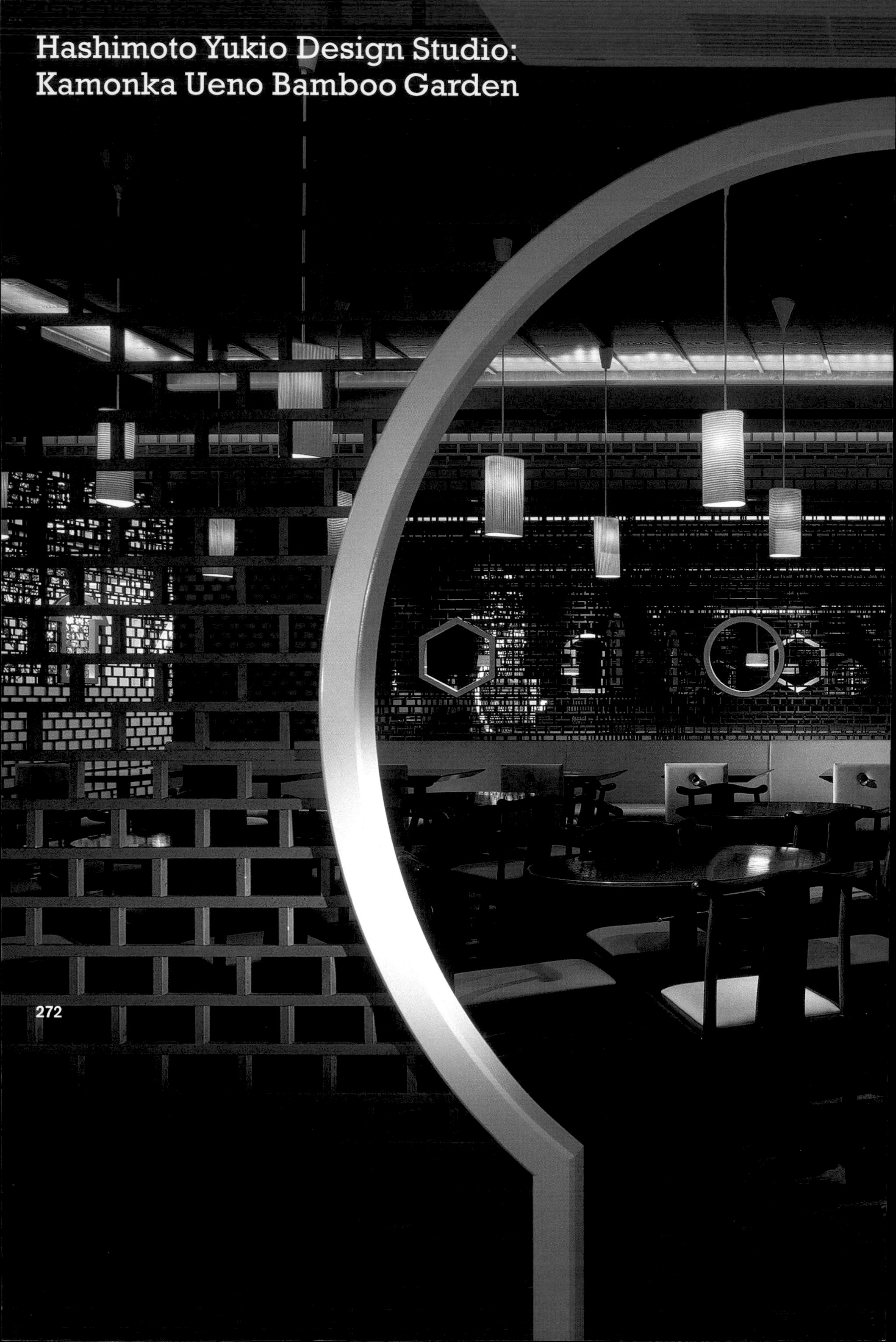

274

Architect:
Hashimoto Yukio
Design Studio

Project:
Kamonka Ueno Bamboo
Garden

Location:
Tokyo, Japan

Year of completion:
2005

Architect: Hashimoto Yukio
Design Studio
Project: Kamonka Ueno Bamboo Garden
Location: Tokyo, Japan

Text by Masaaki Takahashi
Photography by Nacása & Partners

The entrance to a restaurant and the passage from entrance to dining room is enhanced by the expectation of a good meal in relaxing surroundings. Yukio Hashimoto, a master in the design of elegant restaurant interiors, believes that ushering guests through an attractive entrance and along a well-considered path to the place where their food will be served is the most important element of his plan. 'Its significance can be understood when you think of how much the introduction of a novel or a movie seizes your heart,' says Hashimoto. 'The passage holds many subplots and sometimes paints a picture of how the story of the visit will end.' In Hashimoto's interiors, the entrance and the pathway to the dining room symbolize the design concept and pique the curiosity. Four Kamonka restaurants exemplify his words.

The central passage of Kamonka Ueno Bamboo Garden is the backbone of the restaurant, which specializes in Sichuan cuisine. It occupies the ground floor of Bamboo Garden, a building adjacent to the gigantic Ueno Station, gateway to the northern part of Tokyo. The building features three exclusively designed restaurants: Chinese (ground floor), Japanese (first floor) and Korean (second floor).

Preceding spread: Mirrors on the wall look like windows.
Opposite: LEDs have been used to illuminate the series of keyhole arches that welcome guests to the restaurant.

Left: The glazed façade is adorned with the image of a dragon.
Right: Kamonka Ueno Bamboo Garden includes six distinctive dining areas.

Kamonka's entrance passage consists of a series of illuminated keyhole-shaped arches that emphasize the long perspective. Flanking the corridor and extending from the entrance to the rear of the space are an open kitchen, which is situated to the left as one enters the restaurant, and, to the right, a dining area hemmed in by latticed walls with a masonry motif. Resembling wood, the brown walls are made from painted steel and are intended to generate the sense of privacy provided by a bamboo grove, while allowing diners a glimpse of what is going on around them. Latticed partitions screen off certain areas of the open-plan restaurant without producing a noticeable feeling of compartmentalization. The room next to the kitchen, which differs from the rest of the space, features white walls and Chinese lanterns made from translucent acrylic.

Hashimoto says he incorporated LEDs into the series of arches that welcome guests to the restaurant, adding that the shape of this 'array of gates' was 'derived from Chinese patterns'. Even more specifically, he attributes the concept to his impression of the gates and openings of a building he saw at Yuyuan Garden while visiting Shanghai. Yuyuan Garden was built 400 years ago by a Ming bureaucrat named Pan Yunduan, who presented it as a gift to his parents. Now a tourist attraction, the garden – with its bridges, pavilions and walled arbours – invites visitors to escape the hustle and bustle of Shanghai. Viewed through ancient Chinese windows, the garden offers a different scene from every angle. Hashimoto says he felt as if the garden were made not by human design but from God's point of view. He believes that the Chinese artists and craftsmen of the Ming Dynasty poured all their talent into achieving perfection down to the tiniest detail, while never losing sight of the big picture. And he introduced the same exquisite style to the interior of Kamonka Ueno Bamboo Garden. 'Nowadays, architects and designers from all over the world gather in Shanghai to express their individual styles, but I think people are forgetting the beauty that lies in Chinese tradition.'

Architect:	Project:	Location:	Year of completion:
Hashimoto Yukio Design Studio	Kamonka Ueno Bamboo Garden	Tokyo, Japan	2005

明

里 留 半 酔

Opposite top: Although they look like wood, the latticed walls are made from steel.
Opposite bottom: The room next to the kitchen features white walls and Chinese lanterns made from translucent acrylic.

This page: Yukio Hashimoto designed the tables and chairs shown here.

278

Architect:
Hashimoto Yukio
Design Studio

Project:
Kamonka Ueno Bamboo
Garden

Location:
Tokyo, Japan

Year of completion:
2005

Translating the beauty of tradition into contemporary interiors – and revelling in the resulting contrasts – is Hashimoto's forte. He uses words like 'super' and 'surreal' in describing the way he feels about centuries-old Chinese design, which he considers a rich artistic resource for today's designers. And he reminds us that in creating places where people meet, the interior architect should clarify the character of the venue. This rule applies even more strongly, he says, to restaurants. 'It's the personality of the space that appeals to people – just as they would be drawn to the personality of a man.' The focus can be on the space itself, on the food, on the chef, or on all three. 'The place will never be interesting unless its character is clear. At the same time, people who go out to eat expect to be entertained.

Entertained but not overwhelmed. Too much entertainment quickly becomes boring.' He mentions Disneyland as 'an archetype of something so perfectly customer-orientated that it not only attracts people but encourages them to return again and again. The character of the facility and of its service is quite clear and understandable' (all of which does not mean that Hashimoto is a fan of Disney design). In addition to personality and character, he stresses the importance of a restaurant interior that has a pleasant atmosphere in which diners can relax. 'It takes less than 15 minutes to find out whether or not a place is comfortable.' At Kamonka Ueno Bamboo Garden, it takes no more than a few steps.

YUKIO HASHIMOTO BELIEVES THAT USHERING GUESTS THROUGH AN ATTRACTIVE ENTRANCE AND ALONG A WELL-CONSIDERED PATH TO THE DINING ROOM IS THE KEY TO GOOD RESTAURANT DESIGN.

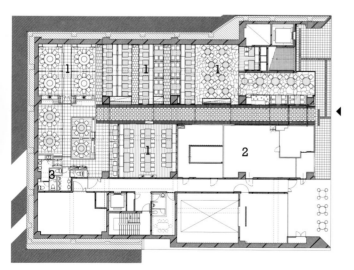

Floor plan
1 Dining area
2 Kitchen
3 Lavatories

Opposite: The entrance to a restaurant is crucial to the impression that the designer is hoping to make on the future clientele.

16 OZ PCHOP BRAND APPLE CINNA SAUCE

ORK

ITH

Y

ION

Slick Design & Manufacturing: Carnevor

Architect:
Slick Design & Manufacturing

Project:
Carnevor

Location:
Milwaukee, USA

Year of completion:
2005

Architect: Slick Design & Manufacturing
Project: Carnevor
Location: Milwaukee, USA

Text by Sarah Martín Pearson
Photography by Zaitz Photography

A trio of seasoned restaurateurs has provided Milwaukee, Wisconsin, with a 21st-century steakhouse. Unsurprisingly, Carnevor is nestled snugly near their other establishments on one of the city's main thoroughfares, Milwaukee Street. Omar Shaikh, Tom Wackman and Demetri Dimitroulous called in another trio – Rocco Laudizio, Amanda Bertucci and Robert Ibarra of Slick Design & Manufacturing – to give the interior of Carnevor a look to match the concept they had in mind: a restaurant reflecting the rustic image evoked by a menu featuring meat, fish, poultry and game, from filet mignon to Cornish hen to crab cakes, accompanied by side dishes of fresh vegetables, a select choice of wines and delightful desserts.

Welcoming visitors with an overall golden gleam, the elongated, 603-m² space has been divided into three levels. At the main entrance, a robust timber door gives way to the core dining area and to a glinting golden bar zone. An impressive array of bowed beams covered in artificial bark hangs overhead like the ribs of some primitive beast. Backing the bar are liquor cabinets of transparent amber acrylic resin, lit from the edges. This display of bottles has been integrated into a wall covered with glossy, gold-vinyl panels framed in squares of espresso-tinted wood.

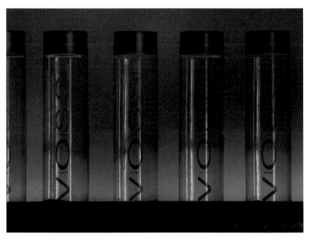

285

Preceding spread and opposite: The elongated, 603-m² space is spread over three levels. Seen on the photograph is the main dining area and its central bar zone. Halogen floor lighting bathes golden vinyl walls in a warm glow.

Left: Suspended from the ceiling are curved beams covered in artificial bark. Light penetrating these timbers can be compared to sunbeams filtering through an arched pergola.
Right: Lit from within, liquor cabinets behind the bar are made from transparent amber acrylic resin.

Sunken into the matching ash flooring are amber-filtered halogen lamps, which send beams of light up the walls lining the space to create an exotic, mysterious atmosphere infused with golden sensuality. The rest of the room is dimly lit by ceiling lighting which filters through the curved timbers, imitating the effect of sunbeams pouring through an arched pergola. Furniture matching this chocolaty gilded ambience includes gold-vinyl-upholstered bar seating with square, stainless-steel bases, arranged alongside a bar fronted in the same vinyl, here protected by clear acrylic sheeting. The harmonizing bar counter is made from a slab of Crema Valencia marble. Among the stylish golden stools are a number of rather crude examples whose organic designs employ natural branches and leather-mesh seats. Parts of trees appear throughout the project in items such as custom-made doorknobs, railings, mirror frames and cocktail tables. Most striking, however, is the suspended cedar-branch partition screen that adds a touch of privacy to the upper-level dining area.

The lowest level, decorated with contrasting accents of golden knotty pine and acid-etched concrete, houses a pool table with all-round seating and yet another dining area, in the form of several tables along the perimeter of the room. Here, as in all areas of the restaurant, purpose-designed tables have espresso-tinted wooden tabletops and black, powder-coated, tulip-type bases. Chairs are upholstered in brown leather. The call of the wilderness permeating this space through the use of natural materials – marble, leather and wood, including rough branches and bark – both combines and contrasts with the contemporary lifestyle referred to by the sophisticatedly synthetic appeal of vinyl, acrylic and neon. In line with today's rectilinear, minimalist school of thought, all elements blend together in a stylish entity that is undeniably au courant. The aesthetics of the design fuse an imaginary primitive world and a civilized, up-to-date environment, turning basic objects from nature into chic items and predatory instincts into a unique dining experience.

Architect:	Project:	Location:	Year of completion:
Slick Design & Manufacturing	Carnevor	Milwaukee, USA	2005

Opposite top: Along the gleaming golden bar are vinyl-upholstered stools with square, stainless-steel bases. These stools are a striking contrast to the organic designs of other stools, also at the bar, that combine natural branches with leather-mesh seats. The bar front is covered in the same gold vinyl, here protected by clear acrylic sheeting.

Opposite bottom: A detail of the rustic rest room shows a conical, stainless-steel basin and, covering the length of one wall, a branch-framed mirror.
This page: The colour scheme includes chocolaty hues with a golden gleam, espresso tints and black accents.
Tables were designed especially for Carnevor. Materials borrowed from nature are in counterpoint to synthetic elements used in the interior.

Golden surfaces reminiscent of luxurious fabrics and Asian handicrafts conjure up an exotic fantasy. At the same time, gold dresses the scene with an opulence and a sophistication that are enhanced through the creative use of light against a dark backdrop. Organic materials recalling a primal world of ethnicity, however, bring the diner back to reality, as does food that – according to Marc Bianchini, culinary consultant at Carnevor – is simple in its focus on the glorious flavours of animal protein, despite its often elaborate presentation.

As the team at Slick points out, 'In a town thriving on change, passionate about style and in desperate need of edgy design, this project was the ultimate reinvention of the steakhouse, a neo-medieval banquet hall for those who relish the challenge of exotic meats.' The designers sum up their take on the interior design from the viewpoint of the visitor to Carnevor: 'Patrons, who push open the massive wooden entry door are guided into the space by captivating golden and chocolate hues and devoured by the intense character of the restaurant, minimal in its expanse, modern in its aesthetics, muscular in its massive rectilinear lines, and unashamedly masculine in its demeanour.'

'IN A TOWN THRIVING ON CHANGE, PASSIONATE ABOUT STYLE AND IN DESPERATE NEED OF EDGY DESIGN, THIS PROJECT WAS THE ULTIMATE REINVENTION OF THE STEAKHOUSE.'

Slick Design & Manufacturing

288

Architect:	Project:	Location:	Year of completion:
Slick Design & Manufacturing	Carnevor	Milwaukee, USA	2005

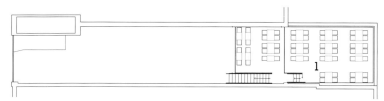

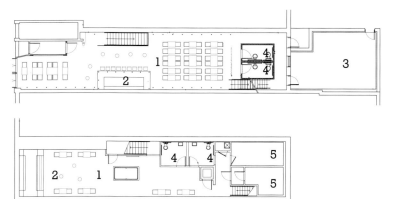

Floor plans
1 Dining area
2 Bar
3 Kitchen
4 Lavatories
5 Storage

Above: View from the upper level of the dining room through a suspended cedar-branch partition screen which enhances the double height of the space while adding intimacy to this area.

Stefan Zwicky Architects and Müller und Fleischli: Food Hall Globus du Molard

294

Architect: Stefan Zwicky
and Müller und Fleischli

Project:
Food Hall Globus du Molard

Location:
Geneva, Switzerland

Year of completion:
2004

Architect: Stefan Zwicky and
Müller und Fleischli
Project: Food Hall Globus du Molard
Location: Geneva, Switzerland

Text by Anneke Bokern
Photography by Oliver Schuster

Generally speaking, department-store restaurants
are not the most inviting places. One might think
that the cold, conventional design and lukewarm
food are simply a ploy to get customers scurry-
ing back to the sales floors as quickly as possible.
That the restaurant might be the main objective
of visitors to the department store is scarcely
considered.

The new Food Hall at Globus, a department store
on Place du Molard in Geneva, proves the pos-
sibility of another approach, however. Globus is
a Swiss chain of stores, proud of its long tradition
and a resonant motto: 'Savoir Vivre'. Up-market
goods displayed in a distinguished atmosphere
range from clothing, home furnishings and beauty
products to fine foods from the delicatessen.
According to Stefan Zwicky, 'all the stores occupy
prime central sites. Globus in Geneva, for
instance, is surrounded by jewellery shops.'

Every Globus store has a delicatessen with an
adjoining restaurant. Two Zurich-based architects,
Stefan Zwicky and Stefan Müller, have worked
together on the design of several of these temples
of gastronomic delight. Their collaboration
has produced restaurants with an assertive,
distinctive look. Zwicky attributes this 'unified
image' to the continuity of their teamwork.

Opposite: The architects designed the dark-stained
oak tables, which have a slot for serviettes, pepper
mills and sauce bottles.

Left: At night sliding doors separates the department
store from the Food Hall.
Right: Island hobs and flooring are in the same matte-grey
colour. Red walls draw attention to the hobs.

The Food Hall in Geneva is linked aesthetically, in terms of colours and materials, to all Globus restaurants created to date. But it does feature one entirely new concept, as it is the first with no table service. Guests go to one of seven island hobs to fetch the meal of their choice. The menu includes sushi, noodle dishes, panini and crepes. Initial preparation of the dishes takes place in a central kitchen, situated in the basement alongside the delicatessen. Diners watch the final touches being given at one of the islands. 'The organization of the islands was quite a challenge,' says Zwicky. 'Nuisance factors like odours, noise and rubbish had to be well regulated so that customers were not inconvenienced.' At the same time, the islands form a focal point – a balance between the bustling atmosphere of a self-service restaurant and the calm elegance generated by the minimalist design of the space.

Some of the hobs are accessible from all sides. Others line the walls. Bar stools at island counters, larger tables in the middle of the dining area and small groups of tables around the islands vary the visual impact of the space and offer a good choice of seating. A broad, straight line leading from the street entrance on the square into the department store continues on a diagonal path through the room, separating the two larger islands. Here the customers' comings and goings intersect, as the Food Hall is one of the three main entrances to the store. The layout may seem like a recipe for collisions, but it is part of a conscious strategy to establish a lively atmosphere and to give the restaurant the feel of the city.

The target group for the Food Hall restaurant is composed of Globus shoppers, passers-by with a clear view of the facility through large display windows, and diners who have made a special trip to eat at this particular restaurant. Zwicky says the Food Hall functions as an 'interface between the department store and the outside world'.

296

| Architect: Stefan Zwicky and Müller und Fleischli | Project: Food Hall Globus du Molard | Location: Geneva, Switzerland | Year of completion: 2004 |

297

Opposite: Grey terrazzo tiles cover the floor.
Red walls and food being prepared at the hobs
provide flashes of colour.

This page: At the panini bar, even the simplest
sandwich has the look of a delicacy. Suspended halogen
lamps create a metropolitan atmosphere.

Des paysages diversifiés et des microclimats favorisent, en Suisse, l'épanouissement de produits de première qualité. Dans les villes et les villages. Dans les fermes, les fromageries, les boucheries, les boulangeries. Dans les plaines et dans les vallées, sur les collines et les montagnes. Avec la confiance dans les traditions et dans l'innovation.

★★★
delicatessa
Globus

298

Architect: Stefan Zwicky
and Müller und Fleischli

Project:
Food Hall Globus du Molard

Location:
Geneva, Switzerland

Year of completion:
2004

Then, too, longer opening hours – the store closes at eight and the restaurant at midnight – underline the independent nature of the restaurant. Enabling this division of functions are sliding glass doors, which close off the retail section of the complex after eight.

'The Food Hall restaurant is designed so that customers can sit at their leisure, not just snatch a quick snack,' says Zwicky. Proving his point is an elegant, minimal interior that makes diners feel comfortable when prolonging their stay. Deep red walls contrast with light-grey floor tiles, dark-stained oak furniture and charcoal-grey metallic panelling on the ceiling. Apart from the walls, it is food being prepared on island hobs that provides the colour. Clever spotlighting brings out the vivid hues in dishes viewed against a dark background. Spotlighting is also used in this way in the delicatessen.

Tables designed by the architects involved in the project are coupled with La Palma chairs modified to be the perfect height for bar tables. Diners visible in their seats have an excellent view of the teeming restaurant. 'The motto is "See and be seen",' says Zwicky. 'On the one hand, the view from both inside and outside is unrestricted because of the huge windows. On the other hand, an important part of the concept is the view around the restaurant itself, made possible by the extra-high chairs and tables. What's more, we chose to display the dishes in beautiful glass cases, before the extravaganza of their final preparation on the island hobs.'

'THE FOOD HALL RESTAURANT IS DESIGNED SO THAT CUSTOMERS CAN SIT AT THEIR LEISURE, NOT JUST SNATCH A QUICK SNACK.'

Stefan Zwicky

Floor plan
1 Sushi / Sashimi
2 Panini / Tapas / Antipasti
3 Coffee / Wine Bar
4 Crépes / Glaces

5 Boulangerie Artisanala
6 Bakery
7 Welness Bar
8 Entrance department store
9 Lavatories

Opposite: The recipe for the design of the Food Hall is the Swiss love of straight lines combined with the succulence of red. La Palma chairs were custom-made to achieve the desired height.

ROASTED KING PRA[WN]
WRAPPE[D] COLONNA[TA]
SERVED [S]ALAD AN[D]
GREENS

302

303

304

Architect:
Leigh & Orange

Project:
Isola Bar & Grill

Location:
Hong Kong, China

Year of completion:
2004

Architect: Leigh & Orange
Project: Isola Bar & Grill
Location: Hong Kong, China

Text by Edwin van Onna
Photography by William Furniss
and Jolans Fung

With over 650 m² of floor space, Isola Bar & Grill may be Hong Kong's largest Western-style restaurant. It's at Isola that the business crowd gathers for the antipasti buffet, tea on the terrace and 'happy hour' cocktails followed by dinner. Responsible for the serene interior of this Italian restaurant (owned by the Va Bene Group), with its splendid view of Victoria Harbour, is Hugh Zimmern of Leigh & Orange Architects. The key elements of his design are light and its effect on textured surfaces.

Zimmern was not out to create 'a signature destination restaurant'. Leigh & Orange had previously designed restaurants for the Va Bene Group, including Gaia and Va Bene restaurants in Hong Kong, Hangzhou and Shanghai. Unlike the Ferrari-red interior of Gaia and the classic Tuscan atmosphere at Va Bene, Isola's largely white environment is distinctively contemporary. The concept took its cue from the location: Isola occupies Levels 3 and 4 of the IFC Mall on Hong Kong Island. The city-side view is dominated by skyscrapers, including a towering building featured in the film Tomb Raider. The view of the harbour, however, is a 270° panorama, complete with piers, ferries and the skyline of Kowloon.

305

Preceding spread: View from the paved outdoor terrace showing the exclusive chill-out bar and Victoria Harbour.
Opposite : Wooden doors and a wall of bottles at the entrance extend a warm welcome to visitors. The Isola logo was designed by Lilian Tang.

Left: The chic lounge on the fourth floor of the shopping mall is a fully glazed box with striking LED lighting.
Right: A steel canopy with a laser-cut filigree motif by Lilian Tang heightens the sense of intimacy in this part of the restaurant.

The existing architecture of the mall – remarkable, to say the least – might have posed a considerable problem for the interior architect. Determining the form of the restaurant are long, whimsically shaped spaces and slanted walls that influence both the height of the interior and the floor plan. Furthermore, four heavy concrete columns prevent long views and interfere with circulation. Zimmern remained unflustered by such restrictions. 'The plan was quite easy to derive and was based on the maximization of the harbour view.' He's referring to the highlight of Isola: the unique view of the water beyond breathtaking windows that stretch from floor to ceiling. In the pair of third-level dining rooms, as well as in the chic lounge, Leigh & Orange has literally drawn the harbour into the restaurant. To soften the experience after sundown, when the scene might have overwhelmed diners, Zimmern installed several types of artificial lighting. 'As the bar box is almost fully glazed, a lot of lighting comes in at night from the surrounding buildings,' he says. 'The steel columns have colour-changing LED uplights. Above them is a line of spot-lit mirror balls.'

Isola has one of Hong Kong Island's few outdoor dining facilities. Spacious terraces at both levels allow for alfresco dining made even more intimate by an overhanging roof. The granite-tile flooring of these terraces extends a short way into the dining rooms. 'We brought the external granite floor partially into the dining rooms to diffuse the glass line and to create more of an outside dining experience for those sitting inside,' says Zimmern. 'The rest of the floor is in reclaimed pine.'

Those entering the restaurant from the mall are greeted by experienced cooks who demonstrate their culinary talents in a series of open kitchens. Here, in a simple, rustic space, young star chef Gianni Caprioli bases his menu on fresh produce and traditional ingredients. The kitchen island, with its butcher-block counters, acts as a buffer between the restaurant and the shop-lined walkway outside.

306

Architect:	Project:	Location:	Year of completion:
Leigh & Orange	Isola Bar & Grill	Hong Kong, China	2004

307

Opposite top: In the rest room, the guest encounters a space with blood-red walls displaying a crocodile-skin motif.
Opposite bottom: The lacy patterns on the canopy inside the restaurant are repeated in the relief featured on a semicircular entrance wall of whitewashed concrete blocks.

This page: A white canopy adorned with silhouettes of vines and frolicking figures forms an enchanting setting for a relaxing meal.

Architect:
Leigh & Orange

Project:
Isola Bar & Grill

Location:
Hong Kong, China

Year of completion:
2004

'We wanted the feel of a stand-alone restaurant,' says Zimmern. A striking semicircular entrance wall of whitewashed concrete blocks with a relief pattern functions as a transition zone and offers a taste of what is to come. Eschewing colour, the architect welcomed light pouring in through the enormous glazed façade with a serene interior and white furniture. 'The light during the day is very strong, and I felt that any colour would be bleached out. Therefore the use of white.' He says they used 'texture and shadow to create interest', alluding not only to the entrance but also to a secluded dining area enhanced by an ornamental canopy. A white plafond of 3-mm sheet metal shelters the diners like a baldachin, suggesting a covering of lace rather than metal. The laser-cut filigree motif traces a silhouette on wall and ceiling. 'I wanted something between a 3D wallpaper pattern and 18th-century silhouettes,' explains Zimmern. Graphic designer Lilian Tang, who also crafted Isola's logo and menu, designed enchanting scenes featuring plant life and frolicking figures: a motif that appears on both canopy and concrete relief wall. To emphasize the secluded ambience of a small VIP room, Zimmern designed a sliding screen into which he incorporated flattened stainless-steel pans, beaters and kettles. Their glistening silhouettes hover in midair, underlining Isola's reputation as an open-kitchen establishment.

Adjectives like 'serene' and 'enchanting' do not tell the whole story, however. With several Island Martinis under his belt, the guest who makes his way to the toilet enters a space where blood-red walls display a crocodile-skin motif. Toilets nearer the lounge are equally surprising, with their glazed, water-filled ceilings. A visit to the loo can be a hallucinatory experience after a relaxing in-terval on the terrace with the harbour at your feet.

'I WANTED SOMETHING BETWEEN A 3D WALLPAPER PATTERN AND 18TH-CENTURY SILHOUETTES.'

Hugh Zimmern

Opposite and above: Incorporated into the sliding screen that Tang designed to separate the main dining area from a small VIP room are flattened stainless-steel pans, beaters and kettles.

Mueller Kneer Associates:
The Cotton House

830m²

314

Architect:
Mueller Kneer Associates

Project:
The Cotton House

Location:
Manchester, England

Year of completion:
2004

Architect: Mueller Kneer Associates
Project: The Cotton House
Location: Manchester, England

Text by Edwin van Onna
Photography by Rolant Dafis

Visitors to The Cotton House on Ducie Street in Manchester might be expecting all the industry-related activity linked to a cotton warehouse. Apart from the name, however, the only hint of the restaurant's industrial past is in its raw brick and cast-iron architecture. Nowadays, bales of cotton and toiling labourers have given way to open spaces, shiny floors, lipstick-red surfaces and relaxed guests. London architecture firm Mueller Kneer Associates has converted 800 m² of this Victorian warehouse into an entertainment venue complete with restaurant, lounge and champagne bar, and the accompanying general and technical services.

The concept features a sequence of interconnected spaces. Visitors moving from one to another can lounge in comfortable bucket-seat chairs by Johanson in the bar downstairs; sip champagne at mezzanine level while enjoying a clear view of the entrance; or dine in the labyrinthine restaurant, which offers classic British fare prepared with fresh produce from local markets by chefs Neil Morris and James Ashton. While sauces simmer and oven-hot bread cools in the kitchen, homemade ice cream goes into the freezer to reach perfection overnight.

Preservation of existing architecture was high on the client's list of requirements.

Preceding spread: Red carpeting in the dining room, a product of Milliken Carpets, makes a striking contrast to the floor downstairs, a gleaming expanse of resin-topped concrete by Altro. Opposite: Stylish Panton chairs manufactured by Vitra embellish the dining room.

Left: A black box hovering among the 19th-century cast-iron columns accommodates the lounge and champagne bar.
Right: The mezzanine, where ring-shaped ceiling lights complement lounge furniture by Johanson.

The building once belonged to a series of warehouses that were vital to the large-scale cotton-processing industry that gave Manchester the nickname 'Cottonopolis'. Most of these warehouses did not survive the 20th century wave of deindustrialization. One exception is The Old London Warehouse, which numbers among its new functions an apartment-style hotel, offices and The Cotton House. The original cast-iron skeleton – still considered an innovative solution in the 19th century – is a clearly visible part of the new design. The architects were also keen to preserve the brick vaulting and metre-thick walls.

Responding to the unrefined architecture, Mueller Kneer introduced soft, contemporary elements into the interior. Partner Olaf Kneer on the conscious separation of styles: 'This is partly a heritage strategy, as the building is protected by the conservation department. The industrial shell is clad with a soft, folded space – one distinction between old and new. The rawness is part of the heritage; we wanted to show that, not erase it, without being obliged to match it. Instead, we wanted to set against it something quite fine and precise. We also felt the need to provide comfort to guests, hence the soft, fine materials.'

Illustrating his words is the restaurant, with its 6-m-high ceiling, monumental cast-iron columns and labyrinth of theatrically tasselled 'curtains'. Long, white fringes hanging from the ceiling surround black table-and-chair, stopping just above the tabletops and creating a sense of privacy without blocking the diner's view of the remaining space. Taking their cue from this organic layout are stylized polyurethane Panton chairs and organically shaped black-leather banquetes.

Mueller and Kneer's preference for a spatial, architectonic design for The Cotton House is seen in their treatment of the vast, open interior. 'Spaces of this size, like airports or shopping malls, can be overpowering,' says Kneer.

Architect:
Mueller Kneer Associates

Project:
The Cotton House

Location:
Manchester, England

Year of completion:
2004

Opposite top: In the dining area, a labyrinth of 'curtains' by Ardo consists of long, white fringes whose total length is an impressive 120 m – a virtual forest of swaying Hawaiian skirts.

Above: Dominating the mezzanine level is an interplay of old and new: the original metre-thick brick walls of the building versus the soft, contemporary elements that Mueller Kneer added to the existing space.

'We wanted to avoid that and create intimate areas, but without losing the generosity.' Inspired by The Situationist International, a mid-20th century political and artistic movement with explicit ideas on urban planning, the architects designed a sequence of atmospheric 'quarters'. 'One of the main techniques of the Situationists is the "derive", which is a kind of "drifting" through the city from one ambient unit to the next,' explains Kneer. 'Within the space we tried to set up zones, but without physical boundaries, each with its own experiential qualities. We wanted people to drift through the space from one quarter to another.'

Nonetheless, the old warehouse is not a maze of cubicles. A single architectonic element determines one's experience of the space: a two-floor vertical box with openings. This black block contains back-of-house functions – toilets, kitchen, staff rooms, storage areas – in addition to the lounge and champagne bar, while separating such functions from the restaurant. Because daylight enters the building only through the side windows of the former warehouse, rings of CCFL tubes have been built into the ceilings of the box. The resulting reflection of indirect but bright light on white ceilings is a pleasant imitation of daylight.

The idea of 'a house in a house' gives an ambiguous twist to the way inside and outside are perceived. 'You enter the restaurant space,' says Kneer, 'but you are still outside the house we inserted.' An interesting aspect is that wherever the box opens, its lipstick-red 'entrails' appear, thanks to the use of glossy laminated wall panelling and a red-glass partition bordering the kitchen. Part of the mood-making strategy, red was chosen for its stimulating effect on guests.

'Red increases human metabolism by 13 per cent.' Conclusion: eat at The Cotton House and burn enough calories to make place for a dish of the chef's delectable homemade ice cream.

318

'SPACES OF THIS SIZE CAN BE OVERPOWERING. WE WANTED TO AVOID THAT AND CREATE INTIMATE AREAS, BUT WITHOUT LOSING THE GENEROSITY.'
Olaf Kneer

Architect:	Project:	Location:	Year of completion:
Mueller Kneer Associates	The Cotton House	Manchester, England	2004

Lamital HPL panels on the walls of the stairwell wear a coat of glossy red paint.

319

322

324

Architect:
PrastHooft Architects

Project:
Brasserie Harkema

Location: Amsterdam,
Netherlands

Year of completion:
2003

Architect: PrastHooft Architects
Project: Brasserie Harkema
Location: Amsterdam, Netherlands

Text by Edwin van Onna
Photography by Jeroen Musch
and Gillian Schrofer

Viewed from the quiet alley outside, Brasserie Harkema in Amsterdam looks like a Cyclops. A deep, broad, counter-like window in the dark façade is the sole link with the interior of the former tobacco warehouse, which currently accommodates a restaurant dominated by light and tranquillity. A rainbow of colour streams down one wall of a space topped by enormous skylights. Responsible for the cosmopolitan design are Dutch architects Herman Prast and Ronald Hooft. 'After discussing the project with the client,' says Hooft, 'we saw a large-scale, approachable restaurant as our best option.' Rather than an unvaried interior, they wanted an international environment with the flavour of Amsterdam: a place both simple and convivial, both grand and cosy. The result is a harmonious whole made up of differentiated parts that allow guests to choose between the openness of the main dining room and the seclusion of the lowered dining area, the bar or the skybox.

The brasserie takes its name from Harkema Tobacco Merchants, which occupied the premises until early 2001. Nowadays, Nes Street – the aforementioned lane and once the tobacco centre of Amsterdam – is home to a string of theatres.

Preceding spread: The 'floating' platform at the entrance continues as a stairway (made from 5-mm-thick steel) to the mezzanine.
Opposite: A broad window interrupting an otherwise blind façade visually opens the restaurant to the street. The style of this original façade is Amsterdam School, which developed in the early 20th century.

Left: The structural wall bordering the kitchen is covered in acoustic material and hides behind a rack with rectangular openings for storing wine bottles.
Right: Soft northern light enters the restaurant through the sawtooth roof, filling the space with a sense of serenity.

In the renovated Harkema building, the tang of tobacco leaves has made way for the aromatic culinary delights of chef Rob Hofland, who previously ran the kitchens at Koriander and Het Gemaal. During the day, his staff of 13 serves up simple dishes and homemade pastries. The evening menu offers classic fare with few frills.

PrastHooft tore down the existing interior and redesigned the entire space, leaving intact or restoring several existing elements, such as the pine flooring and the sawtooth roof above the area once used for selecting tobacco leaves. Filling the space is the soft northern light that made that job easier and now enhances the dining experience at Harkema. Skylights that would otherwise appear as dark holes after sundown have been fitted with colour-changing LEDs. And a linear-lighting system of spots illuminates the tables.

The high-ceilinged dining hall is furnished economically with birch chairs and the architects' purpose-designed tables.

'We chose the chair for its archetypal look – a chair that could have been drawn by a child,' says Hooft. A great sense of spaciousness emerges from the winding, multifunctional structure that unfolds throughout the interior. A volume of wood and steel, it covers the entrance like a canopy, metamorphoses into a 'floating' platform, continues as a stairway to the skybox and ends as a wardrobe on the upper floor. The skybox is a glazed void that welcomes up to 40 guests and boasts a DJ booth, a logical feature of a restaurant whose owner, Michiel Kleiss, has worked as a DJ. 'Extra insulation in the room upstairs allows for a higher decibel level,' says Hooft. 'Behind a black, translucent curtain is an acoustic wall clad in cellulose fibres and illuminated by a stroboscope.'

Intimate spaces are not reserved for the first floor. Separating a cosy, oak-veneered bar at ground level from the large dining room is a theatrical, metal-beaded curtain. 'Not only did we want to differentiate the bar area from the rest of the space in terms of material,' says the architect.

326

Architect:
PrastHooft Architects

Project:
Brasserie Harkema

Location: Amsterdam,
Netherlands

Year of completion:
2003

Opposite: A rhythmic arrangement of plywood chairs and Corian tables welcomes diners to the alcove beneath the skybox.

Above: To mute unwanted noise in an aesthetic manner, PrastHooft Architects clad certain surfaces in cellulose fibres, thus creating a interesting texture, and built the rainbow wall out acoustic panels by Bruynzeel, which were handpainted on the spot.

328

Architect:
PrastHooft Architects

Project: Harkema

Location: Amsterdam,
the Netherlands

Year of completion:
2003

'We also used the lowered ceiling to conceal mechanical systems.' Less sexy material-related solutions were chosen for the lowered dining area which, stripped of all plaster- and paint-work, recalls an exposed archaeological site. Walls of cement-bonded particleboard and bare light bulbs emphasize the coarse texture of the acoustic ceiling. The structural wall in the kitchen, hidden behind a handsome floor-to-ceiling wine rack, has been similarly treated. Bordering the large open kitchen, the rack is perforated with rectangular openings for the bottles. 'Although the building offered plenty of space elsewhere, the client wanted a special place for storing wine,' says Hooft, adding that the wall was inspired by stacked pallets. The role played by acoustics at Harkema is essential but not conspicuously so, thanks to the aesthetic interpretation of this function. Who would guess, for example, that the rainbow wall – with its hand-painted stripes in 118 hues – is composed of acoustic panels by Bruynzeel?

Earlier work by PrastHooft can be seen in the impressive interiors of hospitality-related venues such as Zento, New Deli, Seymour Likely, Hotel Arena, Escape and Sinners. 'But we consider Harkema our most successful hospitality project,' says Hooft, who reveals that his firm will be extending the restaurant with three chambres separees, rooms designed for groups of eight, 12 and 50 guests. The extension will occupy the adjacent building, purchased especially for this purpose. Preparations include measures for the preservation of the premises. 'Two of the chambres have received a listed status; existing wainscoting may not be removed. We'll try to implement the Harkema style in these rooms, while observing all restrictions.' Fortunately, experience has taught these architects that limitations can open the way for innovation.

SKYLIGHTS IN THE SAWTOOTH ROOF ABOVE THE AREA ONCE USED FOR SELECTING TOBACCO LEAVES BATHE THE SPACE IN THE SOFT NORTHERN LIGHT THAT MADE THAT JOB EASIER AND NOW ENHANCES THE DIN-ING EXPERIENCE AT HARKEMA.

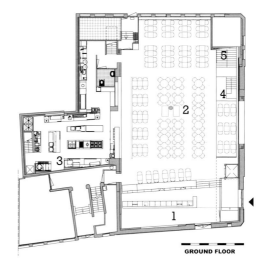

GROUND FLOOR

Floor plan
1 Bar
2 Dining area
3 Kitchen
4 Stairs to lavatories
5 Stairs to skybox

Opposite: The entrance area has a cheerful exuberance that is enhanced by a rainbow wall of hand-painted stripes.

LANZO
CHEESE
FONDUE
BLACK
OIL AND
CROUTO

OMA

WITH

RUFFLE

NS

Simone Micheli:
P Food & Wine

334

Architect:
Simone Micheli

Project:
P Food & Wine

Location:
Turin, Italy

Year of completion:
2006

Architect: Simone Micheli
Project: P Food & Wine
Location: Turin, Italy

Text by Sarah Martín Pearson
Photography by Maurizio Marcato

A restaurant that piques the curiosity: what does the P stand for? The clue lies in the name of the client, the Region of Piedmont, which commissioned the design of P Food & Wine to serve visitors to the 2006 Winter Olympic Games in Turin, Italy. As the temporary occupant of a spacious palace, the restaurant had a dual function: to feed guests and to show off local products – exhibited in contemporary display cabinets – within a stylish environment. In an attempt to engage all the senses, architect Simone Micheli aimed for a carefully choreographed experience composed of light, sound, motion, taste and smell. In his lyrical description of the result, he calls the restaurant 'a three-dimensional manifesto of the marriage between architecture and food design' and a fusion of the 'conceptual and absolutely functional furnishings and food that appear as culinary art'.

Black and white elements featured in the architect's 'total design', a term he uses to emphasize that he put his stamp on everything from furniture and table linens to the uniforms, hair styles and make-up of the staff. Shapes and materials formed a harmonious ensemble with little variation, thus providing a global sense of visual unity.

335

Preceding spread and opposite: Randomly dispersed throughout the space are sleek, organic-shaped poufs upholstered in black fabric. Provided with small aluminium trays, these versatile seats are ideal for informal snacking at the bar.

Left: Products from the Piedmont region fill contemporary display cases integrated into black-laminate partitions that resemble screens. The cases are illuminated to stand out against the dark elements enclosing them.
Right: Black furnishings are silhouetted against a pale background bathed in constantly changing coloured light.
Photography by S.M.A.H.

Glossy volumes and surfaces with a black laminate finish stood out against a white veil of organza curtains, lit from behind. These curtains draped the walls, injecting a sense of weightlessness into a dining room firmly anchored by the organic shapes of sleek black tables, chairs and display cases spread randomly throughout the space, all speaking the same volumetric language. Along the ceiling, a serpentine strip of neon lamps illuminated the curtains, drenching the fabric in a soft fuchsia hue. A row of LEDs tracing the perimeter of the room dispersed light of the same colour onto the aluminium-panelled floor. The lights gradually brightened and dimmed, generating an illusion of movement that was enhanced by a gentle breeze from concealed air jets, bringing the curtains to life. A double layer of organza enveloped the staircase, which – although a solid architectural element made of tempered glass and stainless steel – gave the impression of an ascent enclosed in a vaporous space. 'It is a temporary installation, ephemeral but true architecture,' Micheli said of his project. 'The spaces are treated as fragments of architecture, not just volumes to be furnished.' And into these spaces he poured a distinct and dramatic dose of self-expression 'that communicates with the senses at all levels'.

Guests entered the restaurant, which covered two floors, through the main entrance of the palace, which faces the Piazza del Castello. Flanking the doorway and providing information were two 'wheeled totems'. A black laminate frame gathered the curtains at each side of the door. Sculptural furnishings were key players in distinguishing the various sections of the restaurant, which began with a bar close to the entrance. Seating in this area comprised a series of comfortable poufs upholstered in black fabric, complete with small aluminium trays that held drinks and snacks from the bar.

Architect:	Project:	Location:	Year of completion:
Simone Micheli	P Food & Wine	Turin, Italy	2006

Opposite top: In the dining area, trapezoidal tables with gleaming black tops are combined with shiny, black-wicker chairs.
Opposite bottom: The theme of black and white shadows continues on rest-room doors featuring human silhouettes – images that seem to be projected onto the white surfaces.

Above: A white veil of organza curtains, lit from behind, drapes the walls, adding a sense of weightlessness to the dining room. A combination of neon lamps along the ceiling, LEDs tracing the perimeter of the floor and curtains reflecting changes in the intensity of coloured light playing on the fabric creates a unique yet subtle light show.

Ground floor

First floor

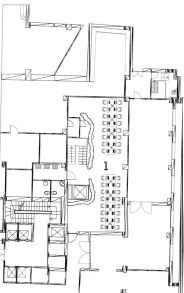

Basement

338

Architect:
Simone Micheli

Project:
P Food & Wine

Location:
Turin, Italy

Year of completion:
2006

Continuing towards the stairwell, one found a larger dining area, where trapezoidal tables with gleaming black tops and round, stainless-steel bases were complemented by chairs with tubular chrome frames and shiny, black-wicker seats. Of the two display cases located at this level, one, with built-in lighting, contained objects suspended on nylon thread, and the other, equipped with a 51-cm monitor, concealed the kitchen and services area.

The upper level began with a lobby, also furnished with poufs, and ended in the VIP dining room. Here, too, the architect used a monitor integrated into a black laminate wall to conceal the services area. The lobby lent access to an outdoor terrace covered by a ceiling panelled in black laminate. Arching down from ceiling to wall, each panel was equipped with a monitor, lighting and fuchsia LEDs.

At P Food & Wine, function joined creativity, and the outcome was a dramatic space that moved to the rhythms of colour, light, sound and images. Add the vital sense of taste and the aroma of Italian cuisine to this equation, and the inevitable result was the total sensory experience that Micheli set as his goal while envisioning the completed project. His theatrical interventions brought the space to life, attracted customers and invited guests to interact with their surroundings while savouring the delicacies of Piedmont. For some, the restaurant underlined the Olympic atmosphere of ice, snow and chill winter weather – a feeling reinforced by 'athletic silhouettes' on toilet doors and the sporty, streamlined forms of Micheli's black furnishings. All in all, his design was a gift for the senses at a world sporting event whose hosts were hoping to offer visitors a memorable taste of the 'big P' in a unique setting.

THE RESTAURANT IS 'A THREE DIMENSIONAL MANIFESTO OF THE MARRIAGE BETWEEN ARCHITECTURE AND FOOD DESIGN.'

Simone Micheli

Floor plan
1 Dining area
2 Bar
3 Lounge

SEA BAS
BREADE
A PIQUA
NUT CRI
SERVED
LIGHTL
SPINAC

343

Architect:	Project:	Location:	Year of completion:
IDing	Odeon	Amsterdam, Netherlands	2005

Architect: IDing
Project: Odeon
Location: Amsterdam, Netherlands

Text by Anneke Bokern
Photography by Teo Krijgsman
and Ron Offermans

For years, the Odeon Theatre in Amsterdam led a somewhat shadowy existence. A popular disco and concert venue in the '80s, it was almost reduced to ashes in 1990, after which it grew increasingly decrepit. When gastronomy entrepreneur Paul Hermanides bought the huge canalside building in 2003, it was clearly in need of a complete overhaul. His aim was to convert the dimly lit disco with its tatty basement rooms into an attractive restaurant, brasserie, club, concert hall and lounge.

Enter Sanne Schenk and Tommy Kleerekoper of Amsterdam-based IDing, designers who had previously done the interiors of a hotel and club for Hermanides. The new project brought them face to face with an interior designer's worst nightmare. The Odeon, erected as a brewery in 1662 and later converted into Amsterdam's first concert hall, is a listed building whose basic structure may not be altered in any way.

Schenk, Kleerekoper and Hermanides made a virtue of necessity by including the history of the building in their design and by opting for an unconventional spatial arrangement. For example, the bar is not in the basement but on the mezzanine, and the brasserie, where breakfast and lunch are served throughout the day, is in the somewhat sepulchral basement.

345

Opposite: The cocktail bar occupies what was formerly known as 'the period room'. Wall panels created by photographer Michel Olden are modern allegories for the four seasons.

Left: The dominant feature of the basement brasserie is wood. The designers inserted mirrors between the old oak beams to lighten the room.
Right: White chairs and a white-tiled floor contrast with the red-brick walls of the brasserie.

346

The Spiegelzaal ('Hall of Mirrors'), a space situated at the heart of the building and once used as the concert-hall foyer, became the restaurant. The designers have uncovered the glamorous, old-fashioned charm of the concert hall well hidden by layers of renovation and restoration, emphasizing their discoveries with heavy curtains, large mirrors, warm colours and many an ironic twist. This is best seen in the mezzanine cocktail bar, a formerly ostentatious space that now radiates an air of cool kitsch. In a previous life, this was the period room, a prestigious space with high windows and sumptuous wall and ceiling paintings. IDing had permission to change only the wall panels, which were not part of the original building. Many designers would have used the opportunity to take a minimalist approach, in an attempt to soften the ornate jewellery-box effect of the room. IDing, however, asked photographer Michel Olden to create neo-baroque interpretations of the ceiling paintings, which depict the seasons.

Olden's work, which graces the walls of the bar and outstrips the paintings in terms of pathos, would not be out of place in a glossy fashion magazine. Nowadays at the Odeon, his larger-than-life, partially clothed beauties look down on guests sipping Caipirinhas.

Adjoining the bar is the restaurant, currently divided into a golden area and a red area and furnished with unobtrusive, contemporary furniture. High mirrors alluding to the history of the room combine with curtains – an intriguing mix of diaphanous, billowing, heavy and voluminous fabrics – to create an atmosphere reminiscent of Versailles, or Versailles in the minds of sober Dutch citizens. Think minimalism with a touch of luxury.

347

Opposite: Black and red give the Odeon a feel of luxury. Plump Mollie chairs are by Allermuir.

Above: The restaurant is in the old Hall of Mirrors. An abundance of fabric – ceiling drapery, flounced curtains and Romeo Soft lamps by Flos – make the vast room more intimate.

From the restaurant, a broad staircase at the back of the building leads to the grand salon and to the lounge on the upper floor, as well as to the brasserie in the basement, which can also be accessed directly from the street.

The brasserie extends a different sort of welcome. No velvet curtains and sophisticated surfaces here. Brick walls and untreated wood speak the language of the underground. 'It doesn't matter whether it gets dirty,' says Kleerekoper. IDing stripped the large room down to the bare bones to establish a distinct contrast between this space and the high-end aesthetic of the rest of the building. The designers were not out to create a shoddy dive, however. The brasserie, which opens at 11 a.m. and remains open all day, has a shiny floor, a mirrored ceiling, silver neo-baroque lamps, and comfortable sofas that coil round the columns in this part of the building – all features that are intended to brighten the atmosphere. It was no easy undertaking, but the Odeon's listed status made it impossible to site the brasserie anywhere else in the building. Spending a sunny, summer afternoon in a basement café may not sound like such a great idea, but with all the cool, rainy weather in the Netherlands, it's less of a problem than one might think.

IDing has given each space at the Odeon – sumptuous bar, glossy restaurant, raw brasserie – a distinctive atmosphere, stemming in part from the history and original function of the building. One amusing reference to the past is in the rest rooms, where Schenk and Kleerekoper have placed armchairs from the Smoke series by Dutch designer Maarten Baas, who uses a torch to burn traditional furniture until all surfaces are matte black, before finishing the pieces with epoxy resin. 'They have actually been charred,' says Sanne Schenk. 'It fits beautifully with the fact that, twice in its history, the building has almost burned down.'

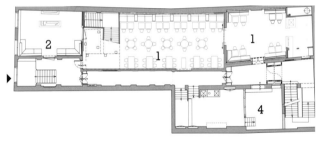

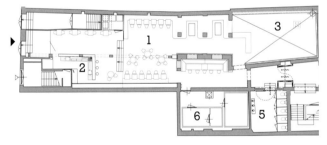

348

Architect:
IDing

Project:
Odeon

Location:
Amsterdam, Netherlands

Year of completion:
2005

349

Floor plan
1 Dinning area
2 Bar
3 Kitchen
4 Cloak room
5 Lavatories
6 Storage

In the basement, Allermuir's Mollie chairs and Container tables by Moooi are mirrored on the ceiling. The wood-panelled wall contains a slot for newspapers.

GRILLED
STEAKS
WITH P
YELLOW
AND YUZ

Andrés Escobar & Associés:
Duvet

354

Designer:
Andrés Escobar & Associés

Project:
Duvet

Location:
New York, USA

Year of completion:
2004

Designer: Andrés Escobar & Associés
Project: Duvet
Location: New York, USA

Text by Carolien van Tilburg
Photography by Jerry Ruotolo

Eating, lounging and dancing in bed – in reviewing the hip nightlife of New York City, that's what young restaurateur Sabina Belkin found lacking. Having already made a name for herself as the co-owner of several Brazilian-style restaurants, she felt that New Yorkers needed something new and innovative. She approached interior designer Andrés Escobar for his help in converting the Centro-Fly club into a cooler-than-cool complex combining restaurant and lounge. The plan for Duvet was under way.

Montreal-based Escobar took one look and found that the premises needed a unique feature. He wanted something 'impressive' that would enhance New York's 'beloved happy hour', the early-evening period in which bars and clubs offer drinks at reduced prices. Escobar suggested adding an illuminated bar to the 'upscale dining while reclining' concept. The Ice Bar is the first thing that catches the eye of visitors entering from Manhattan's bustling West 21st Street. Taking centre stage in an open space, it is surrounded by 34 seats. The handcrafted, rough-textured glass bar is lit from within by colour-changing LEDs. A series of acrylic tables nearby also features LEDs, which change colour in sync with those integrated into the bar.

355

Preceding spread: Satin-covered cushions filled with goose down add to the comfort and luxury of bedroom dining. Bags and shoes are stowed in handy drawers beneath the mattresses.
Opposite: Guests are invited to eat and dance in bed. Small plastic tray tables keep drinks from spilling, and all 30 mattresses are made from a special type of foam that stabilizes any movements made by diners.

Left: Diners have a good view of other guests while also enjoying the privacy provided by translucent Lycra-and-nylon curtains.
Right: Acrylic-resin bar tables visually enlarge the bar area, while also distinguishing this zone from the rest of the restaurant.

These tables serve as focal points, visually enlarging the bar area. 'They are like communal pods, diverting the crowd from the bar,' explains Escobar. 'When it's really crowded, they come in handy for standing at and parking drinks.' Sharing the space with the Ice Bar is the frosted-glass Amuse Bar, which seats ten and serves appetizers such as sushi, tapas and caviar. A glass sculpture against the rear wall in this area was the result of an accident. 'While we were installing the glass bar, one part broke,' recalls Escobar. 'We redefined it as a piece of art by combining it with silver-painted wood. It's a nice contrast to the clean, sleek environment.'

From the bar area, guests have a view of enormous 'dining beds' adorned with dozens of satin pillows. Together with Lycra-and-nylon curtains, they evoke images from The Book of One Thousand and One Nights. The pearly touch reflects the lights in a nice way and gives unexpected dimensions to the lighting.' For Escobar, the lighting system was crucial in creating a glamorous, comfortable ambience. He asked XS Lighting & Sound to program and install the CK LED system, which provides easy-maintenance, energy-friendly lighting and generates no excess heat. The outfit installed 256 metres of LEDs in the Ice Bar alone, adding LEDs wherever possible throughout the restaurant to further embellish the ingenious lighting system. Thanks to the extremely long life of LEDs, glass components used in bar, stair treads and pod tables were able to be completely enclosed. In a brightly illuminated space 'all the fine details have to be perfect.

Cool glass juxtaposed with soft mattresses and a scattering of gold and beige satin pillows provides another nice contrast. Foam mattresses – on 30 beds – mould to the reclining body. Doughnut-shaped discs at the centre of each bed keep drinks from tipping over, and food is served on trays.

Designer:
Andrés Escobar & Associés

Project:
Duvet

Location:
New York, USA

Year of completion:
2004

357

Opposite top: Taking centre stage is a genuine eye-catcher: an illuminated bar with seating for no fewer than 34 guests. Opposite bottom: Unisex toilets feature centrally positioned washbasins. The view from this space includes the wine cellar.

Above: Bed and bar chair offer a view of an enormous fish tank filled with hundreds of jellyfish whose translucent bodies change colour along with the lighting.

358

Designer:
Andrés Escobar & Associés

Project:
Duvet

Location:
New York, USA

Year of completion:
2004

'If someone is dancing on the mattress, food on another part of the mattress doesn't spill,' says Escobar. Drawers in the base of each mattress hold shoes and bags. Less adventurous guests are shown to small tables lining the periphery of the space.

Floating in an enormous aquarium behind the Ice Bar are more than 100 jellyfish, chosen for their ability to absorb colour. Like magic, their translucent bodies change colour along with the lighting.

After descending an illuminated glass staircase, visitors enter a lounge with seven VIP 'bedrooms' for up to 12 guests each. The basement level also accommodates a unisex rest room and a wine cellar. Toilets exemplify the phrase 'see and be seen'. Seated in the cubicle, the guest is invisible to others yet has a clear view of those washing their hands or applying their make-up. 'Doors with one-way mirrors have a voyeuristic character,' laughs Escobar. 'People using the toilets have the feeling that they're not completely invisible.' They needn't worry, however, as lighting in the cubicles is dimmer than elsewhere in the rest room. The view across from the mirrored doors reveals the contents of the wine cellar.

If an atmosphere of relaxed luxury was the goal, it has certainly been achieved. And an elaborate menu of 'progressive American' cuisine makes Duvet both a visual attraction and a venue pleasing to the taste.

'IF SOMEONE IS DANCING ON THE MATTRESS, FOOD ON ANOTHER PART OF THE MATTRESS DOESN'T SPILL.'

Andrés Escobar

Above: The Ice Bar, which was entirely handcrafted of textured glass, features built-in, colour-changing LED lighting.

Address list

Bon Appétit
Addresses restaurants:

a FuturePerfect
Lane 351 Huashan, House 16,
Huashan Lu
Shanghai 200040
China
T +86 21 6248 8020
F +86 21 6249 4011
www.afutureperfect.com.cn

Client: A.M Therapy
Interior architect: A00 Architecture
Design team: Sacha Silva,
Raefer K. Wallis, Jim Wang, Cindy Xu
Graphic designer: SGTH
Design team: Mario Van Der Meulen,
Mei Ling Tsui
Manufacturers: A00 Architecture, Vitra
Max. capacity: 56 seats (restaurant),
52 seats (terrace)
Total floor area (m2): 120 (restaurant),
130 (terrace)
Total cost (¥): 540,000
Budget per m2 (¥): 2160
Duration of construction: 3 months
Opening: November 2005
Photographers: Gary Edwards, But-Sou Lai,
Shenghui Photography Company

Askew
504 La Guardia Place
New York, NY 10012
USA
T +1 212 529 3560
F +1 212 529 3561
info@askewnewyork.com
www.askewnewyork.com

Client: Edwin Chong
Designer: Karim Rashid
Manufacturers: Kravardt, Magis,
Benjamin Moore, One Shot Florescents,
Puredesign/OFFI, Vanceva Laminates,
Karim Rashid
Duration of construction: 3 months
Opening: November 2005
Photographer: Tom Vack

Buddha Boy
Westfield Shopping Centre,
Church Street, Parramatta
Sydney
Australia
T +61 2 9633 3555
F +61 2 9633 3555

Client: Buddha Boy
Interior architect: Giant Design
Graphic designer: Nerida Orsatti Design

Manufacturers: Abet Laminates,
Décor Panels, IDC, ISM
Max. capacity: 40 seats
Total floor area (m2): 65
Total cost (€):142,952
Budget per m2 (€): 2200
Duration of construction: 3 weeks
Opening: December 2005
Photographer: Andrew Worrsam

Café Blanc
ABC MALL
Beirut 2612-6002
Lebanon
T +96 1121 1120
F +96 1121 1119
jp@cafe-blanc.com
www.cafe-blanc.com

Client: Café Blanc Lebanon
Interior architect: George Henry
Chidiac Architects
Graphic designer: Maria Dolores
Mouraccade
Max. capacity: 185 seats
Total floor area (m2): 670
Total cost ($): 900,000
Budget per m2 ($): 1350
Duration of construction: 5 months
Opening: July 2005
Photographer: Imad el Khoury

Carnevor
724 North Milwaukee Street
Milwaukee, WI 53202
USA
T +1 414 223 2200
F +1 414 223 2203
www.carnevor.com

Client: Thomas Wackman Group
Interior architect: Slick Design &
Manufacturing
Design team: Amanda Bartucci,
Robert Ibarra, Rocco Laudizio
Graphic designer: Bitcrafter Media
General contractor: ADK Designs
Consultant: Caren Crangle,
Jeff Hojniack, Rocco Laudizio
Manufacturers: ADK Designs, Commercial
Custom Seating, Elk Grove II, E&T Plastics,
Fishman Fabrics, Granite and Marble
Resources, Old Hickory, Seabrook
Wallcoverings, Sandler Seating,
Super Duper Games,
Rareform Unique Archtectural Products
Total floor area (m2): 603
Total cost ($): 600,000
Budget per m2 ($): 995
Duration of construction: 3 months
Opening: December 2005
Photographer: Zaitz Photography

Ciné Città
C-Mine 1.1 (Euroscoop)
3600 Genk
Belgium
T +32 89 3638 85
F +32 89 8619 47
maria@cine-citta.com
www.cine-citta.com

Client: Ciné Città
Interior architect: Puresang
Manufacturers: CEP furniture, Luyten
Max. capacity: 200 seats
(restaurant), 20 seats (bar)
Total floor area (m2): 300
Total cost (€): 500,000
Budget per m2 (€): 1200
Duration of construction: 5 weeks
Opening: November 2005
Photographer: Kristien Wintmolders

Dahlberg
Stortorget 20
25222 Helsingborg
Sweden
T +46 42 1243 44
info@gastropub.nu
www.gastropub.nu

Client: Per and Sara Dahlberg
Interior architect:
Mental Industrial Design
Design team: Niklas Madsen,
Hans Johansson
Graphic designer: Clas Håkansson
Consultant: FLUX (lighting)
Engineer: Sjödin Fastigheter
Manufacturers: Exakt Snickeri,
Krebs Stockholm, Modular Lighting
Instruments, NC Möbler, Niklas Madsen
Max. capacity: 30 seats (restaurant),
10 seats (bar)
Total floor area (m2): 80
Duration of construction: 4 months
Opening: May 2006
Photographer: Fredrik Segerfalk

Delicabar
Le Bon Marché Rive Gauche,
Espace Mode Femme, 1st floor
26, rue de Sèvres
75007 Paris
France
T +33 1 4222 1012
www.delicabar.fr

Client: Helene Samuel
Interior architect: Claudio Colucci Design
Total floor area (m2): 130 (restaurant),
136 (terrace)
Opening: 2003 (restaurant), 2004 (terrace)
Photographer: Francesca Mantovani

Duvet
45 West 21st Street
New York, NY 10010
USA
T +1 212 989 2121
F +1 212 989 2107
inquiry@duvetny.com
www.duvetny.com

Client: Edward and Sabina Belkin
Interior architect: Andrés Escobar
& Associés
Consultant: XS Lighting & Sound
Manufacturers: Color Kinectics, Télio
& Cie, Think Glass, Red Lion Design,
XS Lighting & Sound
Max. capacity: 1200 guests (night club)
including 300 seats (restaurant)
Total floor area (m2): 2137
Opening: December 2004
Photographer: Jerry Ruotolo

El Bosque de Samsung (ephemeral
project, Casadecor 2005 Barcelona)
Casa Burès, C/ Ausiàs Marc 30-32
08010 Barcelona
Spain
T +34 93 2211 000
www.casadecor.es

Client: Arola-Ritz Catering
Interior architect: Estudio Minim
Vilá & Blanch
Consultants: Samsung Electronics
Manufacturers: Cappellini, Dada,
Gaggenau, Molteni, Samsung, Viabizzuno
Max. capacity: 70 seats
Total floor area (m2): 280
Total cost (€): 111,000
Budget per m2 (€): 392
Duration of construction: 2 months
Opening: November 2005
Photographer: Stephan Zaurig

Food Hall Globus du Molard
Rue du Rhône 48
1204 Geneva
Switzerland
T +41 22 3195 050
F +41 22 3195 088
www.globus.ch

Client: Globus Genf
Interior architect: Stefan Zwicky,
Müller und Fleischli
Project Manager: Markus Santschi
Consultant: Enerconom, Promafox, Scherler
Engineers: Fellrath & Bosso
Manufacturers: Agencement Steiner, Jegen
Max. capacity: 180 seats
Total floor area (m2): 710
Total cost (€): 5,088,000

Budget per m2 (€): 7100
Duration of construction: 5 months
Opening: October 2003
Photographer: Oliver Schuster

Glass
Vicolo del Cinque 58
00153 Rome
Italy
T +39 06 58335903
www.glass-hostaria.com

Client: Glass
Interior architect: Andrea
Lupacchini Architect
Design team: Andrea Lupacchini,
Sveva Giovagnoni, Monica Masini,
Gianluca Garofalo, Ugo Lezziroli
Graphic designer: Marco Filippetti
Consultant: Alberto Trabucco,
Fabio Spada, Silvia Sacerdoti
Manufacturers: Animart Service,
Alberto Brandolini
Max. capacity: 100
Total floor area (m2): 190
Duration of construction: 1 year
Opening: June 2005
Photographer: Beatrice Pediconi

Brasserie Harkema
Nes 67
1012 KD Amsterdam
Netherlands
T +31 20 4282 222
info@brasserieharkema.nl
www.brasserieharkema.nl

Client: Brasserie Harkema
Interior architect:
PrastHooft Architects
Graphic designer: Hotel
Engineers: Duyts Bouwconstructies
Manufacturers: A&D interieurs, Baxmeier, Lente,
Max. capacity: 250 seats
Total floor area (m2): 900
Duration of construction: 9 months
Opening: October 2003
Photographers: Jeroen Musch,
Gillian Schrofer

Hitsuji
1-115 Iguchi, Tenpaku-ku
Nagoya 468-0052
Japan
T + 81 52 801 1240

Client: Wasabi Co
Interior architect: Torii Design Office
Graphic Designer: TYPE A/B
Engineers: Yoshitake
Manufacturers: Y+
Max. capacity: 69 seats

Total floor area (m2): 146
Duration of construction: 1 month
Opening: November 2005
Photographer: Nacása & Partners

Isola Bar & Grill
Level 3 & 4, ifc Mall, Central
Hong Kong
China
T +852 2383 8765
F +852 2383 8622
contactus@vabenegroup.com
www.isolabarandgrill.com

Client: Gaia Group
Interior architect: Leigh & Orange
Graphic designer: Lilian Tang Design
Max. capacity: 300 seats
Total floor area (m2): 770
Total cost (€): 770,000
Budget per m2 (€): 1000
Duration of construction: 8 weeks
Opening: May 2004
Photographers: Lester Lim,
Jolans Fung, William Furniss

Kamonka Ueno Bamboo Garden
Bamboo Garden 1F,
1-52 Ueno Park, Taito-ku
Tokyo 110-0007
Japan
T +81 3 5807 2288
F +81 3 5807 2275
www.kamonka.jp

Client: Ramla Co
Interior architect: Hashimoto Yukio
Design Studio
Engineers: AIDEAL CO
Manufacturers: Bell Furniture
Max. capacity: 270 seats
Total floor area (m2): 579
Duration of construction: 4 months
Opening: April 2005
Photographer: Nacása & Partners

Kantinery
Plange Mühle 1
40221 Düsseldorf
Germany
T +49 211 5858 7770
F +49 211 5858 7758
mail@gcs.info
www.gcs.info

Client: GCS Event Services Catering
Interior architect: Jason Jenkins &
The Finevibe

Manufacturers: Aida, IKEA, Loods 5,
Michaelis
Max. capacity: 140 seats (restaurant),

50 seats (lounge)
Total floor area (m2): 315
Opening: September 2005
Photographer: Jason Jenkins

Khyber
5th Road, Khar West
Mumbai 400-052
India
T +91 22 2648 9311/6
F +91 22 2648 9317
k_khyber@vsnl.net

Client: Sudheer and Rashmi Bahl
Interior architect: Khosla Associates
Graphic designer: tsk Design
Design team: Sandeep Khosla, Tania Singh Khosla,
Amaresh Anand, Madhavi Choudapurkar, Geetika
Alok, Shruti Chamaria, Mihika Deshpande
Manufacturers: Devi Design,
Metro Enterprises, Smith Interiors,
Welpac Products
Max. capacity: 130 seats
Total floor area (m2): 400
Duration of construction: 4 months
Opening: January 2006
Photographer: Pallon Daruwala

Kittichai
60 Thompson Street
New York, NY 10014
USA
T +1 212 219 2000
thomsixty@aol.com
www.kittichairestaurant.com

Client: Michael Callahan, Huy Chi Le,
Robin Leigh, Jean-Marc Houmard
Interior architect: Rockwell Group
General contractor: Inner Gaze
Manufacturers: Bergamo Fabric,
G + W Design, Indecasa, Inner Gaze,
OK's Flower, Orlando Finishing, Jerry Pair,
Silver Associates, Jim Thompson,
Max. capacity: 120 seats (restaurant),
15 seats (bar), 40 seats (terrace)
Total floor area (m2): 280
Duration of construction: 3 months
Opening: June 2004
Photographer: Eric Laignel

Kushiyaki
Shop 9, Level 12, Langham Place
8 Argyle Street, Mong Kok, Kowloon
Hong Kong
China
T +85 2 3514 4333
F +85 2 2625 1717
kushiyaki@biznetvigator.com
Client: Right Loyal Development
Interior architect: Jason Caroline Design
Design team: Jason Yung, Caroline Ma,

Keith Chan
Manufacturers: Decoration Company ,
Wing Construction
Max. capacity: 84 seats
Total floor area (m2): 106
Total cost ($): 160,000
Budget per m2 ($): 1510
Duration of construction: 3 weeks
Opening: February 2005
Photographer: John Butlin

Linc Styles Café
Nihon Linc Bld. 3F,
6-27 Noborimachi Nakaku
Hiroshima 730-0016 Japan
T +81 8 2511 1800 F +81 8 2227 8100
owada@lincstyles.com
www.lincstyles.com

Client: Linc Styles
Interior architect: Intentionallies
Manufacturers: Yoshichu Mannequin
Max. capacity: 25 seats
Total cost (¥): 40,000,000 (whole project)
Budget per m2 (¥): 201,000 (whole project)
Duration of construction: 5 months
Opening: November 2005
Photographer: Nacása & Partners

McDonald's
Via Fulvio Testi 132
20092 Cinisello Balsamo, Milan
Italy
T +39 2 2423 784

Client: Euroristoro
Interior architect: Costa Group
Graphic designer: Benassi Maurizio
Max. capacity: 280 seats (ground floor),
120 seats (first floor)
Total floor area (m2): 400 (ground floor),
150 (first floor)
Duration of construction: 6 weeks
Opening: June 2005
Photographer: Moreno Carbone

MX
G/F, Nam Tin Building
275 King's Road, North Point
Hong Kong
China
T +852 2578 9629
www.maxims.com.hk
Client: Maxim's Fastfood
Interior architects: Steve Leung Designers
and Alan Chan Design Company
Brand consultant: Alan Chan
Design Company
Manufacturers: Art Creation
Lighting Design, B.S.C. Building Material,
Mission Contract Furniture, Spot Light
Max. capacity: 130 seats

Total floor area (m2): 370
Duration of construction: 3 months
Opening: October 2005
Photographer: Ulso Tsang

NuBa
C/ de la Font del Gat 28
08242 Manresa
Spain
T +34 93 8784 390
F +34 93 8784 391
info@grupnuba.com
www.grupnuba.com

Client: Restauració Font del Gat
Interior architect: Francesc Rifé
Manufacturers: Blausmo Santa Coloma,
Cronek, Cristaleria Bonanova,
Decoració Murtra, Dinelectric,
Duravit España, Carpintería Brañas,
Pinturas Murtra, Talleres Colmenero,
Tapisseria Jove, Viccarbe Habitat
Max. capacity: 80 seats
Total floor area (m2): 300
Total cost (€): 270,000
Budget per m2 (€): 900
Duration of construction: 6 months
Opening: December 2004
Photographer: Eugeni Pons

Odeon
Singel 460
1017 AW Amsterdam
Netherlands
T +31 20 521 8555
www.odeonamsterdam.nl

Client: Amsterdam Village Company
Interior architect: IDing
Design team: Tommy Kleerekoper,
Sanne Schenk
Engineers: De Nijs, Heyligers,
Hiensch Engineering, Klik
Manufacturers: Jan Daniëls Interieurbouw,
Frits de Jong, Michel Olden (photos),
Palux, Team Projects, Vertical Vision
Max. capacity: 650
Total floor area (m2): 1700
Total cost (€): 1,600,000
Budget per m2 (€): 940
Duration of construction: 7 months
Opening: April 2005
Photographers: Teo Krijgsman, Ron Offermans

Olio e Pane
Lindenplatz 5
72555 Metzingen
Germany
T +49 71 2338 1161
www.olioepane.de

Client: Holy Ag

Interior architect: RaiserLopesDesigners
Manufacturers: Arper, RaiserLopesDesigners,
Svennson
Max. capacity: 70 seats (restaurant),
70 seats (terrace)
Total floor area (m2): 185 (restaurant),
215 (terrace)
Duration of construction: 9 months
Opening: September 2005
Photographer: Frank Kleinbach

OQO
4-6 Islington Green
London N1 2XA
England
T +44 20 7704 2332
F +44 20 7704 2339
info@oqobar.co.uk
www.oqobar.co.uk

Client: Mark Chan
Interior architect: Hawkins\Brown
Graphic designer: SEA
General contractor: Hawkins\Brown
Structural Engineer: Price and Myers
Services Engineer: Michael Popper Associates
Quantity Surveyor: Appleyard and Trew
Acoustics Engineer: Paul Gillieron Acoustics
Manufacturers: Comren, Viaduct
Total floor area (m2): 150
Total cost (£): 284,000
Opening: December 2004
Photographer: Simon Phipps

P Food & Wine
Piazza castello 165
10122 Turin
Italy
T +39 011 432 3531
F +39 011 432 3280
plounge@regione.piemonte.it
www.piemontefeel.it

Client: Regione Piemonte
Interior architect: Simone Micheli
Manufacturers: Adrenalina, Alfabuilding,
D&A Design & Architettura, Gervasoni,
Gruppo Ragaini, Fabbian Illuminazione,
Isa, Liri Industriale, Silent Gliss, Segno
Total floor area (m2): 1000
Total cost (€): 450,000
Duration of construction: 5 months
Opening: February 2006
Photographer: Maurizio Marcato,
S.M.A.H.

Thaiphoon
Zwartbroekstraat 31
6041 JL Roermond
Netherlands
T +31 47 5333 135
F +31 47 5316 097
info@thaiphoon.nl
www.thaiphoon.nl

Client: Thaiphoon
Interior architect: Maurice Mentjens
General contractor: Tinnemans Bouw Management (TBM), Linne
Manufacturers: 3tac, Barrisol, Camp,
Crespi, Ecophon, Jan Hoven, Rob Huyben,
Interieurbouw Hees, IPC, IT2, Lagotronics,
Madico, Mobles 113, Muurbloem, Uti-licht,
Vitra, Robert Savelkoul
Total floor area (m2): 290
Duration of construction: 16 weeks
Opening: September 2004
Photographer: Arjen Schmitz

The Cotton House
Ducie Street
Manchester M1 2TP
England
T +44 161 2375 052
F +44 161 2375 072
Info@thecottonhouse.net
www.thecottonhouse.net

Client: Paul and Ann Wharton
Interior architect: Mueller Kneer Associates
General contractor: Bridgewater Contracts
Manufacturers: Altro, ABS Contract Furnishers,
HB, Johanson, Walter Knoll, Lamital,
Milleken, Vitra
Max. capacity: 120 seats (restaurant),
70 seats (member's area), 200 seats (bar)
Total floor area (m2): 830
Total cost (£): 825,000
Budget per m2 (€): 993
Duration of construction: 9 months
Opening: November 2004
Photographer: Rolant Dafis

The Hub
Burghley Road
London NW5 1UJ
England
T +44 20 7485 8515
F +44 20 7284 3462
Head@aclandburghley.camden.sch.uk
www.aclandburghley.camden.sch.uk

Client: The Acland Burghley School
Interior architect: SHH Associates
Manufacturers: Formica, Heller,
One Foot Taller
Max. capacity: 175 seats (restaurant),

104 seats (terrace)
Total floor area (m2): 300
Total cost (£): 350,000
Duration of construction: 6 weeks
Opening: September 2005
Photographer: Morley von Sternberg

Thor
107 Rivington Street
New York, NY 10002
USA
T +1 212 796 8040
www.hotelonrivington.com

Client: Hotel on Rivington
Interior architect: Marcel Wanders Studio
Engineers: Grzywnskipons architects
Manufacturers: Cappellini,
Grzywnskipons architects,
Marcel Wanders Studio, Swarovski
Total floor area (m2): 509
Duration of construction: 7 months
Opening: June 2004
Photographer: Inga Powilleit
Photostyling: Tatjana Quax

Trattoria da Loretta
Büchsenstrasse 24
70174 Stuttgart
Germany
T +49 711 2804 507
F +49 711 6494 804
lorettapetti@aol.com

Client: Loretta Petti
Interior architect: Ippolito Fleitz Group
Textile designer: Monika Trenkler
(Wallpaper)
Manufacturers: Einkauf & Logistik,
Konzept Raumausstattung,
Peter Lehner, Massivholz Design,
Sauter Innenausbau
Max. capacity: 42 seats
Total floor area (m2): 85
Duration of construction: 4 months
Opening: February 2004
Photographer: Zooey Braun

Witloof
Bernardusstraat 12
6211 HL Maastricht
Netherlands
T +31 43 3233 538
F +31 43 3233 264
Info@witloof.nl
www.witloof.nl

Client: Ad Fiddelers
Interior architect: Maurice Mentjens
Graphic designer: Suzy Jae
General contractor: Paul Janssen

Manufacturers: Douwe Hoekstra, Rob Savelkoul,
IKEA, IT2, Paul Janssen, Jos Meijers,
Vanessa Verhoeven, Arjen Winterink
Max. capacity: 60 seats
Total floor area (m2): 108
Total cost (€): 90,000
Budget per m2 (€): 833
Duration of construction: 8 weeks
Opening: November 2005
Photographer: Arjen Schmitz

World Hockey Bar
Götgatan 93
11862 Stockholm
Sweden

Interior architect: Abelardo
Gonzalez Arkitektbyrå
Consultant: Aaronsson Byggnads,
Brandkonsulten, Luftkompaniet,
NC-Rör, SEVEKO, TP Fastighetskonsult
Manufacturers: Agabekov, Carisma
Skyltdesign, Design Distrubution,
IDAB Snickerier, Reggiani Lightning,
SSC Skellefteå
Engineers: Electro Engineering,
SWECO, VVS Konsult
Max. capacity: 720 guests
Total floor area (m2): 500
Duration of construction: 6 months
Opening: 2004
Photographer: Åke E:son Lindman

Architects

Bon Appétit
Addresses architects:

A00 Architecture:
a FuturePerfect
1305 Nan Suzhou Lu, 1st Floor
200003 Shanghai
China
T +86 21 6327 6213
F +86 21 6327 6215
mail@azerozero.com
www.azerozero.com

Abelardo Gonzalez Arkitektbyrå:
World Hockey Bar
Västergatan 8
20313 Malmö
Sweden
T +46 40 2325 08
F +46 40 3055 77
info@abelardogonzalez.se
www.abelardogonzalez.se

Alan Chan Design Company
1901 Harcourt House
39 Gloucester Road
Wanchai, Hong Kong
China
T +852 2527 8228
F +852 2865 6170
acdesign@alandesign.com
www.alanchandesign.com

Andrea Lupacchini Architect:
Glass
Via Andrea Pitti 18
00147 Rome
Italy
T +39 6 57 59930
architer@libero.it

Andrés Escobar & Associés:
Duvet
5524 St-Patrick,
suite 400
Montreal H4E 1A8
Canada
T +1 514 2722 131
F +1 514 2725 856
info@escobardesign.com
www.escobardesign.com

Claudio Colucci Design:
Delicabar
4-9-2 Higashi,
Shibuya-ku
Tokyo 150-0011
Japan
T +81 3 5468 5539
F +81 3 5468 5538

36, rue Charlot
75003 Paris
France
T +33 1 4473 0020
F +33 1 4277 3239
contact@colucci-design.com
www.colucci-design.com

Costa Group:
McDonald's
Via Valgraveglia Z.A.I.
19020 Riccò del Golfo
Italy
T +39 01 8776 9309
F +39 01 8776 9308
info@costagroup.net
www.costagroup.net

Estudio Minim Vilá & Blanch:
El bosque de Samsung
Av. Diagonal 369
08037 Barcelona
Spain
T +34 93 2722 425
F +34 93 4883 447
proyectos@estudiovilablanch.com
www.estudiovilablanch.com

Francesc Rifé:
NuBa
Escoles Pies 25
08017 Barcelona
Spain
T +34 93 4141 288
F +34 93 2412 814
f@rife-design.com
www.rife-design.com

George Henry Chidiac Architects:
Café Blanc
Jel el Dib highway Al Arz Bldg 11th floor
El Metn
Lebanon
T +96 1 3572 494
F +96 1 4710 984
gchidiac@gcharchitects.com
www.gcharchitects.com

Giant Design:
Buddha Boy
5, Nicholson street
Crows Nest, NSW 2065
Australia
T +61 2 9906 6940
F +61 2 9906 6191
studio@giantdesign.com
www.giantdesign.com

Hashimoto Yukio Design Studio:
Komonka Ueno Bamboo Garden
4-2-5 Sendagaya, Shibuya-ku
Tokyo 151-0051
Japan
T +81 3 5474 1724
F +81 3 5474 4724
hydesign@din.or.jp
www.din.or.jp/~hydesign

Hawkins\Brown:
OQO
60 Bastwick Street
London EC1V 3TN
England
T +44 20 7336 8030
F +44 20 7336 8851
mail@hawkinsbrown.co.uk
www.hawkinsbrown.co.uk

IDing:
Odeon
Lijnbaansgracht 147
1016 VW Amsterdam
Netherlands
T +31 20 7740 117
F +31 20 4276 546
info@iding.nl
www.iding.nl

Intentionallies:
Linc Styles Café
3F, One eighth Bldg.,
2-18-15 Jingumae, Shibuya-ku
Tokyo 150-0001
Japan
T +81 3 5786 1084
F +81 3 5786 1453
post@intentionallies.co.jp
www.intentionallies.co.jp

Ippolito Fleitz Group:
Trattoria da Loretta
Bismarckstrasse 67B
70197 Stuttgart
Germany
T +49 711 9933 92330
F +49 711 9933 92333
info@ifgroup.org
www.ifgroup.org

Puresang:
Ciné Città
Pacificatiestraat 7
2000 Antwerp
Belgium
T +32 3 2486 455
F +32 3 2486 456
info@pure-sang.com
www.pure-sang.com

RaiserLopesDesigners:
Olio e pane
Hauptmannsreute 69
70193 Stuttgart
Germany
T +49 711 2483 91932
F +49 711 2483 91999
mail@raiserlopes.com
www.raiserlopes.com

Rockwell Group:
Kittichai
5 Union Square West
8th Floor
New York , NY 10003
USA
T +1 212 463 0334
F +1 212 463 0335
spawar@rockwellgroup.com
www.rockwellgroup.com

SHH Associates:
The Hub
1 Vencourt Place
London W6 9NU
England
T +44 20 8600 4171
F +44 20 8600 4181
neilhogan@shh.co.uk
www.shh.co.uk

Simone Micheli:
P Food & Wine
Via Aretina 197R-201R
50136 Florence
Italy
T +39 05 5569 1216
F +39 05 5650 4498
simone@simonemicheli.com
www.simonemicheli.com

Slick Design & Manufacturing:
Carnevor
941 West Randolph street
Chigago, IL 60607
USA
T +1 312 563 9000
F +1 312 563 9008
inquiries@slickdesign.com
www.slickdesign.com

Stefan Zwicky Architects:
Food Hall Globus du Molard
Zweierstrasse 35
8004 Zurich
Switzerland
T +41 44 298 34 00
F +41 44 298 34 01
mail@stefanzwicky.ch
www.stefanzwicky.ch

Steve Leung Designers:
MX
9/F, Block C, Seaview Estate
8 Watson Road, North Point
Hong Kong
China
T +852 2527 1600
F +852 2527 2071
sla@steveleung.com.hk
www.steveleung.com

Torii Design Office:
Hitsuji
Komura Bld. 2F, 31-27 Daikan-cho,
Higashi-ku
Nagoya 461-0002
Japan
T +81 52 933 2878
F +81 52 933 1748
mail@toriidesign.com
www.toriidesign.com

Photographers

Bon Appétit
Addresses photographers:

Zooey Braun:
Trattoria da Loretta
T +49 711 6400 361
F +49 711 6200 393
info@zooeybraun.de
www.zooeybraun.de

John Butlin:
Kushiyaki
T +85 2 9186 3076
arcfoto@netvigator.com

Moreno Carbone:
McDonald's
T +39 335 8307 637
foto@carbonemoreno.191.it

Rolant Dafis:
The Cotton House
T +44 20 8531 5003
rolant.dafis@sothebys.com

Pallon Daruwala:
Khyber
T +91 98 8039 9333
pallond@gmail.com

Gary Edwards:
a FuturePerfect
maxwelledwards@mac.com

Jolans Fung:
Isola Bar & Grill
T +85 2 9779 8151
jolansfung@hotmail.com

William Furniss:
Isola Bar & Grill
T +85 2 9741 2787
wfurniss@mac.com

Jason Jenkins:
Kantinery
T +49 177 7535 726
post@finevibe.com

Imad el Khoury:
Café Blanc
T +96 1 1389 595
info@imadelkhoury.com
www.imadelkhoury.com

Frank Kleinbach:
Olio e pane
T +49 711 6076 731
F +49 711 6076 831
fotografie@frank-kleinbach.de
www.frank-kleinbach.de

Teo Krijgsman:
Odeon
T +31 20 4682 002
fotografie@teokrijgsman.nl
www.teokrijgsman.nl

But-Sou Lai:
a FuturePerfect
T +86 138 1787 5737
photo@butsou.com
www.butsou.com

Eric Laignel:
Kittichai
T +1 917 204 4338
ericlaignel@hotmail.com

Lester Lim:
Isola Bar & Grill
T +85 2 9028 4528
lester@framewerkz.net
www.pbase.com/framewerkz

Åke E:son Lindman:
World Hockey Bar
T +46 8 3435 80
F +46 8 3435 81
ake.eson@fotograf-lindman.se

Francesca Mantovani:
Delicabar
T +33 6 0796 8064
francescammantovani@free.fr
www.francescamantovani.com

Maurizo Marcato:
P Food & Wine
T +39 045 6050 601
F +39 045 6050 146
usmar@tin.it
www.mauriziomarcato.com

Jeroen Musch:
Brasserie Harkema
M +31 6 5024 1662
mail@jeroenmusch.nl
www.jeroenmusch.nl

Nacása & Partners:
Komonka Ueno, Linc Styles Café, Hitsuji
T +81 3 5722 7757
F +81 3 5722 0909
partners@nacasa.co.jp
www.nacasa.co.jp

Ron Offermans:
Odeon
T +31 20 6331 849
ron.offermans@wxs.nl
www.ron-offermans.nl

Beatrice Pediconi:
Glass
T +39 338 4516 069
M +39 06 8559 293
beatricepediconi@alice.it

Simon Phipps:
OQO
T +44 79 7341 4574
simon@simonphipps.co.uk
www.simonphipps.co.uk

Eugeni Pons:
Nuba
T +34 97 2372 505
info@eugeni-pons.com
www.eugeni-pons.com

Inga Powilleit:
Thor
T +31 23 5320 540
F +31 23 5320 724
ingapowilleit@chello.nl

Jerry Ruotolo:
Duvet

Arjen Schmitz:
Witloof, Thaiphoon
T +31 43 3263 194
arjenschmitz@home.nl

Gillian Schrofer:
Brasserie Harkema
T +31 20 535 6210
F +31 20 420 2870
www.concern.nu

Oliver Schuster:
Food Hall Globus du Molard
oliver.schuster@schustervisuell.de
www.schustervisuell.de
T +49 71 1232 403
F +49 71 1236 6168

Fredrik Segerfalk:
Dahlberg
T +46 709 4109 88
info@segerfalk.com
www.segerfalk.com

Shenghui Photography Company:
a FuturePerfect

S.M.A.H.:
P Food & Wine

Morley von Sternberg:
The Hub
T +44 20 8989 5704
F +44 20 8491 1704
morley@vonsternberg.com
www.vonsternberg.com

Ulso Tsang:
MX
T +85 2 2575 6136
F +85 2 2575 6396
ulsotsang@hotmail.com
www.ulsotsang.com.hk

Tom Vack:
Askew
T +49 81 5390 7070
F +49 81 5388 1372
tomvack@t-online.de

Kristien Wintmolders:
Ciné Città
T +32 11 2520 23
F +32 11 2520 23
kristienwintmolders@skynet.be

Andrew Worrsam:
Buddha Boy
T +61 2 9389 7521
F +61 2 9389 7521
andrew@troutesque.com

Zaitz Photography:
Carnevor
T +1 866 210 6186
info@zaitzphotography.com
www.zaitzphotography.com

Stephan Zaurig:
El Bosque de Samsung
T +34 67 0093 025
stephan@zaehring.com
www.maria.com.es

Colophon

Bon Appétit:
Restaurant Design

Publishers
Frame Publishers
www.framemag.com
Birkhäuser – Publishers
for Architecture
www.birkhauser.ch

Compiled by Marlous Willems

Introduction by Shonquis Moreno

Texts by Anneke Bokern,
Shonquis Moreno,
Edwin van Onna, Sarah Martín
Pearson, Chris Scott,
Masaaki Takahashi,
Caroline van Tilburg and
Monica Zerboni

Graphic design
Alvin Chan
www.alvinchan.nl

Copy editing
Donna de Vries-Hermansader

Translation
InOtherWords (D'Laine Camp,
Donna de Vries-Hermansader)
Ella Wildridge

Colour reproduction
Graphic Link, Nijmegen

Printing
D2Print, Singapore

Distribution
ISBN 10: 90-77174-18-4
ISBN 13: 978-90-77174-18-0
Frame Publishers
Lijnbaansgracht 87
1015 GZ Amsterdam
Netherlands
www.framemag.com

ISBN-10: 3-7643-7770-4
ISBN-13: 978-3-7643-7770-0
Birkhäuser –
Publishers for Architecture
PO Box 133
4010 Basel
Switzerland
Part of Springer Science+
Business Media
www.birkhauser.ch

© 2006 Frame Publishers
© 2006 Birkhäuser – Publishers
for Architecture

A CIP catalogue record for this book
is available from the Library of Congress,
Washington D.C., USA

Bibliographic information published
by Die Deutsche Bibliothek
Die Deutsche Bibliothek lists
this publication in the Deutsche
Nationalbibliografie; detailed bibliographic
data is available in the internet
at http://dnb.ddb.de.

Printed on acid-free paper
produced from
chlorine-free pulp. TCF ∞
Printed in Singapore
987654321